passionate faith

passionate faith

Ancient Truths for Contemporary Women

Jennie Afman Dimkoff

Revell
Grand Rapids, Michigan

Published by Fleming H. Revell
a division of Baker Publishing Group
P.O. Box 6287, Grand Rapids, MI 49516-6287

Previously published as *Night Whispers*

Printed in the United States of America

Library of Congress Cataloging-in-Publication Data
Dimkoff, Jennie Afman.
    Passionate faith : ancient truths for contemporary women / Jennie Afman
Dimkoff.
        p.   cm.
    Rev. ed. of: Night whispers.
    Includes bibliographical references (p.   ).
    ISBN 0-8007-5810-2 (pbk.)
    1. Bible stories, English. 2. Christian women—Prayer-books and devotions—
English. I. Dimkoff, Jennie Afman. Night whispers. II. Title.
BS550.3.D56 2005
242′.643—dc22   2005003832

The personal illustrations in this book are true to life and are included with the permission of the people involved. In some cases, names and identifying details have been changed to protect the privacy of the people involved.

This book is lovingly dedicated to my favorite storyteller, Pauline Wielhouwer Afman, better known to me as "Mama."

Dear Mother—How I treasure my childhood memories of your rich contralto voice, weaving stories that wound their way around my young heart. Thanks most of all for sharing the amazing and compelling story of God's love for me. It influenced the course of my life.

Thank you for your unconditional love, your faithful encouragement, and your constant prayer support. I love you.

Contents

Acknowledgments

My dear sister, Carol Kent, who for years has mentored, nudged, and encouraged me to write. Without your example and motivation, I doubt this book would have become a reality.

Dr. Robert Nienhuis, the executive vice president of Cornerstone University, for graciously reviewing my manuscript for biblical accuracy. Thank you, Bob, for lending your intellect and for challenging me to stay true to God's Word.

Marilyn Gordon from Baker Books, who heeded God's prompting and followed up on our conversation at the airport. Without that contact, I doubt I would have found my way to the Baker/Revell publishing family.

Jennifer Leep, my acquisitions editor at Revell. You made this whole project seem possible, and your enthusiasm gave me joy along the way. You were wonderful to work with, and your encouragement always came when I needed it most.

The special friends who allowed me to share their poignant stories (I love you).

Jan Zimmerman, my friend, prayer partner, and traveling companion. Your encouragement, insight, enthusiasm are such a gift to me. Thank you for your help with the Bible study portion of this book.

Linda Goorhouse, whose invaluable help as my office assistant allowed me to meet my deadlines. Your teamwork and enthusiasm made the task far less daunting!

My children, Amber and Joshua, who allowed me to tell their stories and who were cheerleaders, sounding boards, and proofreaders during the process. I'm blessed to be your mom.

My husband, Graydon, who, when I was searching for the right topic, encouraged me to write this book about the stories I love most.

All those who prayed for me during this project! You will never know how much those prayers were needed. Please keep them coming!

How to Use This Book

I love great stories, and the Bible is filled with the very best of the best! In writing this book and retelling ten ancient biblical stories of faith, I desire to invite you to "step within the pages"—to *experience* the stories with the individuals who lived them.

Are you curious about what the Bible has to say to you personally? In each chapter of *Passionate Faith*, you will read a dramatic retelling of an ancient story; a Digging Deeper section to help you understand the culture, politics, and customs, etc.; and a contemporary story that will help you understand and apply the ancient story to your life today.

To get the most out of reading this book, you may want to turn to the back section first, where I have included a ten-week study guide for either individual or group use. For each story of *Passionate Faith*, you'll find five days of individual assignments that will help you to better understand and apply each story to your own life. Some portions of the studies may be more personal, while other parts will lend themselves to meaningful group discussion.

Each week's study will include reading the story, an opportunity to identify the main characters that played a part in the drama, a Scripture reading, a discussion of a major theme in the story, a closer look at the faith of the characters in the story, and application questions to help you become a woman of passionate faith.

Whether you read and review this book on your own or with friends on a weekly basis, consider praying first, asking God to open your mind and heart to the truth that he has for you to gain from your time spent within this book—and more importantly, with him.

Enjoy experiencing *Passionate Faith*! I would love to hear how God uses this book to be a blessing in your life. To share your faith story, email me at jennie@jenniedimkoff.com.

Choosing to trust him,
Jennie Afman Dimkoff

1

A Match Made in Heaven
The First Recorded Love Story

I t was a beautiful, crisp December night, and the young man standing beside me in the observation tower had planned the evening very carefully. As we looked out over the breathtaking beauty of Niagara Falls, with the thunderous roar of the water and the colored lights illuminating the misty cloud that rose up from the base of the falls, he turned, took both my hands in his, and asked me to be his wife.

His question took me by surprise, but I dearly loved the dynamic, poverty-stricken young law student standing before me. With my heart racing and my breath catching in my throat, I responded breathlessly, "I'd love to."

He hesitated a moment. "You will?"

"I'd love to."

There was another hesitation. "You *will?*" he asked again.

This time I clasped *his* hands. Looking into his eyes and nodding my head, I assured him, "Yes! I *love* you, and I would *love* to marry you!"

At that, twenty-three-year-old Graydon Dimkoff swung me up in his arms, twirled me around, and shouted to the people who had just entered the tower, "She loves me, and she just said she'll marry me!"

I love a good love story. Especially those that have surprising facets that keep me glued to them. In fact, I read such a captivating love story recently that I want to recommend the book to you. It's actually a compilation of quite a few stories all in one volume, and after you read the love story I'll be sharing in the following pages, I hope you'll be so intrigued to find out what *else* is recorded in the book that you'll want to take a look yourself.

The book is God's Holy Word, the Bible. And the love story I'm referring to is the story of Rebekah and Isaac. Rebekah's name means "captivating," and she was the Miss America (or rather, the Miss Mesopotamia) of the Old Testament. Her love relationship with Isaac, the son of Abraham and Sarah, begins in Genesis 24, and it's more exciting than a movie script. Will you become a pictorial thinker with me as we step within the pages of the story?

Rebekah's Story

The old man raised a hand to wipe the moistness from his eyes. How he missed her!

Sitting in Sarah's tent brought back a lifetime of memories—her uncommon beauty, their nomadic adventures together, her great sorrow over her years of barrenness, and then her skepticism at the news from God that she would have a child in her old age. Abraham smiled as he remembered their incredible happiness at the birth of their son. They named the child Isaac, which meant "laughter," and the joy he had brought to them in their old age was indicative of his name.

14

At least Sarah lived long enough to see our son grow to manhood, he thought, nodding to himself. Even in his grief, there was much to be thankful for.

Glancing up through the opening in the tent, he saw Isaac walking alone in the field. Studying his son and heir, Abraham sighed. *He grieves for her as much as I do,* he thought. *I have neglected my duty. Isaac is almost forty years old and still single, and I have done nothing to arrange a marriage for him. There is more in life for him than inheriting my estate.*

Pausing to take one last, lingering look around Sarah's tent, the old man summoned his faithful servant to assist him.

"Eliezer, I have trusted you for many years with all that I have. Today I ask you to take an oath to represent me in a matter of great importance. It is time for my son, Isaac, to wed, but under no circumstances do I want him to marry one of the Canaanite women in this land. Do you understand me?"

Nodding, the faithful servant concentrated on every word.

"Come closer to me now and place your hand under my thigh. I want you to swear by the God of heaven and earth that you will not get a wife for my son from the daughters of the Canaanites, among whom I am living. Instead, I want you to journey to my homeland in Mesopotamia to find a wife for Isaac from my own relations. I am far too old to make the journey myself. You must go in my place."

The servant obediently went through the ritual of making the oath, but his mind was racing with unanswered questions. *I am to find a wife for Isaac? I know little about Mesopotamia, and it is a great distance away. How will I know how to locate Abraham's family?*

"I will do as you ask," Eliezer said, "but what if the woman doesn't want to relocate from the city to this country? Should I come back and get Isaac and bring him to Mesopotamia?"

Abraham was adamant. "No! God has promised this land as Isaac's inheritance! God will prepare the way for you, Eliezer, by sending his angel before you. If the woman refuses, you are released from your oath. Swear that you will not take Isaac back there!"

The caravan, which consisted of ten camels packed with rich garments, jewelry, and other bounty of Abraham's wealth, set out. Eliezer set his course for Aram-Naharaim in northern Mesopotamia, specifically for the city of Nahor. The trip was long and arduous, and his heart was heavy with the responsibility before him. After many days he arrived outside the city of Nahor, and he and his men made the camels kneel down near the well that was located there. His arrival was at early evening, the time of day when the young maidens of the town came with their jars to the well for water. His task seemed impossible. Standing there, dusty and tired, Eliezer lifted his heart to God and prayed. "O Lord, God of my master Abraham, grant me success today. I am standing beside this spring, and the daughters of the townspeople are coming out for water. When I say to a girl, 'Please let down your jar so I may have a drink,' and she says, 'Drink, and I'll draw water for your camels, too'—let her be the one you have chosen for Isaac."

A peal of feminine laughter preceded the girl's entrance to the stable where Laban was instructing his servant. "I'm off to fetch the water, brother dear," she announced pleasantly. Inhaling deeply, she cast her eyes outside the stable before bringing them back to rest on Laban. "Isn't it a lovely evening? It's much too nice to stay indoors! I'll be back soon." As quickly as she had come, she was on her way again.

Laban stepped to the door of the stable and grinned as he watched his sister gracefully make her way down the lane, an earthenware jug balanced on her shoulder. *She's a beauty,* he thought and then chuckled. *Yes, she's beautiful, innocent, generous to a fault, and impulsive enough to one day drive a husband to distraction!* Still smiling, he inhaled some of the evening air she had extolled and then turned back to more mundane duties.

Reaching the edge of the town, Rebekah waved to several other girls who were making the same evening pilgrimage to the well, but as she drew closer, her attention was arrested by the sight of ten camels kneeling near the spring. An older man stood slightly apart from the caravan. He was obviously tired and dusty from a long journey, but what caught her attention was that he seemed to be speaking silently—to no one at all.

She lowered her eyes as she passed by him, but was aware that he seemed to be watching her as she filled her jug and raised it with strong, healthy arms to her shoulder once again. As she came back up the path from the well, the man hurried toward her and asked for a drink.

"Certainly," replied Rebekah. Reaching up with both hands, she lowered her jug and tipped it to provide a stream of cool water for the stranger.

As she watched the weary, dusty man drinking thirstily, her young heart was touched with compassion. Without consideration of the great effort it would cost her, she offered, "I'll draw water to fill the troughs until your camels have finished drinking as well."

Without another word, the girl emptied the remaining water into the trough and ran back to the well—again and again—to draw enough water for the entire caravan of thirsty camels.

Eliezer could hardly believe what was happening. Had his prayer been answered so quickly? He watched in silent amazement as Rebekah worked, and after the camels had drunk their fill, he went to his baggage and unpacked a gold nose ring and two lovely gold bracelets. Approaching her with his gifts, he asked, "Who is your father?" Then, sweeping his arm toward the caravan, he added, "Might there be enough room in your home to put us up for the night?"

"My father is Bethuel, and I am the granddaughter of Nahor," Rebekah politely replied. "I'm sure we have plenty of room for you and your men and straw for the camels, too."

She was the one! Eliezer could hardly believe his ears! This beautiful woman was Isaac's second cousin! Without saying a word to Rebekah, he bowed down to the earth and worshiped the Lord in her presence. "Praise be to the God of my master Abraham, who has not abandoned his kindness and faithfulness to my master."

"Mother! Laban! Where are you?" Out of breath from running, Rebekah flung open the door of her mother's house and excitedly repeated what had happened at the well. "Look at the gifts the man gave me!" she exclaimed, showing them the dainty nose ring and glistening golden bracelets.

"Get the house ready and prepare a meal," Laban directed. "I will go welcome our guest!" Laban then hurried to the well, found the man standing near the camels, and invited the man and his company to come home with him.

Still shaken by the events of the day, Eliezer took in the scene around him. Rebekah's father, Bethuel, whom Eliezer knew to be Abraham's nephew, was present, as well as her brother, Laban. Food had been laid before them, but Eliezer was too intent on his mission to eat. "I will not eat until I have told you what I have to say."

Laban responded, "Then speak."

So Eliezer explained that as Abraham's servant, he had been sent to find a wife for his master's son, Isaac, who would inherit all the great wealth of his father. He described how he had sworn an oath, had made the journey, and then had prayed at the well, asking God to point out the right girl. "Before I had even finished my prayer, your beautiful daughter came to the well. When I asked her for a drink, she graciously gave it to me, and then, wonder of wonders, she offered to water the camels! When I discovered that she was from the household of Abraham's relatives, I bowed down and worshiped the Lord."

Eliezer made eye contact with Rebekah for a moment. She was standing in the doorway with a serving dish in her hand and had been listening to his message with widened eyes. She turned back to her father and brother. "Please tell me whether or not you will show kindness to Abraham, so that I may know which way to turn."

Bethuel and Laban looked at Rebekah and then at each other, concurring, "This is from the Lord. Here is Rebekah. Take her and go, and let her become the wife of your master's son."

Too overwhelmed by all she had seen and heard that day to sleep, Rebekah stood in the doorway of her home and stared out into the quiet night, contemplating the future. She had known since she was small that one day her father and brother would arrange a marriage for her. But to leave all that was familiar and go to a distant land was something to think twice about. It was reassuring to her family that the son of Abraham was a rich man, but it was more comforting to her that he had no other wives for her to compete with! Then the sad thought came to her that she would very likely never see her family again.

When it seemed her head would burst with the intensity of her thoughts, she recalled seeing the old man at the well for the first time, and how he had seemed to be praying. She recalled her impulsive offer to water the camels and his astonishing reaction when he learned her father's name. Two more times in her presence she had seen the old man offer a prayer of thanksgiving to God for having led him to her and to her family. The thought came to Rebekah that God had brought them all together, and as she breathed deeply the cool night air, she felt peace wash over her. God was in control, and she would marry a man whose name meant "laughter." She found herself smiling in the darkness.

Early the next morning Rebekah's mother bustled around, directing her servants, her mind full of wedding plans. There was so much to do! There was Rebekah's gown to prepare and her head covering. Friends and relatives would want to congratulate and celebrate with the family. What a shame the wedding couldn't be in Nahor, but she would cherish the time she had left with her daughter and share intimate secrets of the marriage bed with her in the days ahead. So much to do!

Laban and Eliezer came into the room and once again the old man stated what was on his mind rather than choosing to eat first. "I would like to leave and take Rebekah back to my master now."

"What?" Rebekah's mother looked frantically at Laban, who seemed just as startled as she was.

"But you just got here. This is all so sudden. We can't possibly let Rebekah leave on such short notice. We need more time. Give us at least ten days. Then you may take her."

Eliezer was determined. "Please don't delay me any longer. The Lord has granted success to my journey. Send me on my way to my master."

In a dilemma over what to do, they decided to let Rebekah make the decision herself. Calling her into the room, they asked if she would be willing to leave immediately with Eliezer.

Rebekah looked at the family she loved. Then she looked at the man of prayer waiting so expectantly before her, and she replied without hesitation.

"Yes, I will go."

Rebekah hastily prepared to leave her home. Her nurse, Deborah, and her maids would go with her to Canaan, so there was a flurry of preparation. But before she and her maids mounted their camels to leave with Eliezer, her family gathered around and blessed her.

"Our sister, may you increase to thousands upon thousands; may your offspring possess the gates of their enemies."

Swallowing a lump in her throat, Rebekah mounted her camel, waved good-bye to all those she loved, and then turned in her saddle to face the new life that awaited her. The journey would be long, but, she reminded herself, the wedding at the end of the journey would be of divine appointment, and her husband's name meant "laughter."

In the early evening Isaac went out walking in the field to meditate. While his father had embraced a nomadic life, Isaac had a way with farming the land, and the land prospered under his care. He loved to walk in the fields, using the quiet time to think and to pray. Much had been on his mind lately. He had grieved deeply over the death of his mother, but for the past several weeks his conversations with God had centered on the task his father had sent Eliezer to accomplish. Isaac, though wealthy and a man of great importance, was lonely, a godly man living in a pagan land. The thought of a wife who would share not only his way of life, but his faith, brought hope to his heart. Whom would God provide? What would she be like? Plain, but kind? Would he be blessed with a godly woman who was also beautiful, just as his father had been blessed?

Looking up, he saw a caravan coming from the east. Straining to see, he counted ten camels. It must be Eliezer, either with a bride or with the news of her refusal. With his heart thundering, he hurried to meet them.

As the miles passed and the destination drew closer, Rebekah felt an anxious expectation. She turned around to check on her nurse, Deborah, who was weary and saddle sore on the camel plodding steadily behind her own. "We're almost there, Deborah! It shouldn't be long now, dear friend. You may be regretting this trip right now, but I am so very thankful you are with me!"

Turning back to face the westerly trail they were following through land that was more fertile than the desert they had left behind, Rebekah looked up and saw a man on foot, eagerly approaching the caravan. Impulsively, she reined her camel, dismounted, and went to Eliezer to ask if he recognized the man. Indeed, he did.

"It is my master, Isaac!"

She liked what she saw! Isaac was able-bodied and vigorous! With adrenaline racing through her veins, Rebekah took her veil and covered her face properly, indicating her status as an unmarried maiden.

Isaac embraced Eliezer warmly, but his eyes flew past his faithful servant to gaze upon the willowy figure of a woman waiting expectantly behind him. He could see sparkling brown eyes above her veil. The servant eagerly told Isaac the story of how God had led him on the right path to the right woman. Isaac tipped back his head and laughed out loud, clasping the servant's shoulder in gratitude. Then, turning to his bride, Isaac welcomed Rebekah joyfully and brought her to the tent that had been his mother's.

In the absence of Rebekah's mother, Deborah and the other maids prepared Rebekah for her wedding day. Breathtakingly beautiful in her wedding finery, she willingly became the wife of Isaac. Best of all, he loved her, and she was a comfort and solace to him. It was a match made in heaven.

Digging Deeper

Because this romance took place in a culture very different from my own, I had random questions popping into my mind all the way through the story. That was good, because it meant that I had to do some digging in a number of reference books such as commentaries, Bible dictionaries, and books on daily life and culture in Bible times, and I had to check out some maps that showed the journey that Eliezer made to Mesopotamia and back. Let me share some of the fascinating information I found that adds living color to the narrative.

What's in a name? Rebekah's name meant "captivating," and she was just that. Beautiful and strong willed, she kept Isaac "captivated" (as in monogamous) for a lifetime. Isaac and Rebekah lived during a time when polygamy was almost universal, but Isaac never took another wife or indulged in relationships with handmaidens or concubines—even when Rebekah found it difficult to conceive his heir. For the first time in Scripture it is recorded that a man *loved* his wife. And it is not only recorded that he loved her (Genesis 24:67), but there is a reference that much later in their marriage he was still caressing her intimately (Genesis 26:8)!

Isaac's name meant "laughter" or "he laughs." Certainly the title was symbolic of his parents' reaction to discovering they were to have a child in their old age, but I believe the name was also a reflection of his own temperament. Bruce Wilkinson tells of the important connection a man had with his name: "In Bible times, a man and his name were so intimately related that 'to cut off the name' of an individual amounted to the same thing as killing him. A name was often taken as a wish for or prophecy about the child's future."[1]

How much water can ten camels drink? One reference informed me that camels are able to drink approximately nine gallons of water and that they can store enough water internally to last for several days. That made them very valuable transportation and beasts of burden in the desert. If you're doing your math, that means Rebekah could have provided up to ninety gallons for the gangly critters, and Scripture says that she "ran" to do it! (v. 20). (She was a woman of energy and enthusiasm!) Another reference painted a rather vivid picture of traveling via camelback: "Camels traveled in caravans of up to fifteen hundred beasts, groups being roped together and led by a rider on a donkey at about three miles (five kilometers) per hour. . . . The camel was not at all comfortable to ride. It is easy enough to mount when it is in a kneeling (resting) position, but when one rides it, the swaying movement induces travel sickness."[2]

Now we know for certain that Rebekah was a woman of stamina as well as beauty!

An arranged marriage? After Eliezer was assured that the family would part with Rebekah, he unpacked many valuable gifts, including gold and silver jewelry and articles of clothing. Most marriages were arranged, and negotiations were normally made by a representative of the groom (in this case Eliezer). Arranged marriages were also expensive for the bridegroom. "Work compensation [had] to be paid to the woman's family, and a dowry had to be paid to the bride's father. He could use the interest from the dowry but could not spend it because it was to be kept in trust for the wife in case she was ever widowed or divorced. Where such sums of money could not be paid, other means were found instead, such as service, or elimination of enemies."[3]

Would she leave with the stranger? Rebekah had the rare opportunity to choose whether or not to marry Isaac. Because of the unusual circumstances surrounding Eliezer's petition to take Rebekah immediately out of the country, her family decided that she would be given that right. As a twenty-first-century woman, I'm glad. Aren't you? When she chose to go, she went of her own free will.

In Rebekah's culture, the engagement period, or betrothal, which was legally binding, usually lasted for a year, and like today, the bride's family planned the celebration. We know that Rebekah's family did not have the opportunity to plan or even to attend the wedding, but it is very special to note that before she left, they gathered around their daughter and blessed her. What a great idea to incorporate into our prenuptial plans today!

An overview of Rebekah's life reveals significant highlights that you will miss if you only read her love story.

She was barren for twenty years before she had a baby. Childbearing, especially the bearing of sons, gave a woman great significance in Rebekah's culture, and though Rebekah was loved, she experienced humiliation at her barrenness. The pregnancy was a direct answer to Isaac's prayer to God on behalf of his wife (Genesis 25:21).

She had a personal relationship with God. Rebekah talked to God and he talked back! Her pregnancy was difficult, and when she felt an uncomfortable stirring in her womb, the text does *not* say that she went to her midwife for advice. In Genesis 25:22 it says "she went to inquire of the LORD," saying, "Why is this happening to me?"

God spoke to her! He told her that there were two nations at war within her and that the older would serve the younger. We are not told how God spoke to Rebekah, and there is no evidence that she ever told Isaac about her conversation with God.

She had twin boys: Esau, the firstborn, and Jacob. She was the first of only two women recorded in the Bible who gave birth to twins. The boys were as different as night and day and brought bitter conflict into Isaac and Rebekah's family. (Tamar was the other mom of twins in Genesis 38.)

She had a lasting physical beauty. Years after Rebekah and Isaac were married, a famine in the land caused them to move into enemy territory for a long period of time. Isaac was afraid that the men in the land would desire Rebekah because of her great beauty and would kill him if they knew she was his wife. He told her to lie and say she was his sister. One day the king looked down from a window and saw Isaac caressing Rebekah, and the ruse was up! (By the way, Isaac's dad, Abraham, had pulled the same trick with his wife, Sarah, many years before. The apple didn't fall far from the tree—and I think it had a worm in it!)

For all the remarkable and admirable traits that Rebekah possessed, she certainly wasn't perfect, nor were her circumstances always happy.

She favored one child over another. She loved Jacob more than Esau (Genesis 25:28).

She grieved over the two Hittite women her son Esau married. Rather than bring her joy, her pagan daughters-in-law disgusted her (Genesis 27:46).

She lowered herself by tricking her husband. When Isaac was old and blind, she schemed with their son Jacob to trick Isaac into giving Jacob his brother Esau's birthright. It worked, but at what cost? That's a remarkable story in itself.

There is no reference to her death. Her husband, Isaac, lived to be 180 years old.

How can this story apply to your life?

Prayer is important. The servant, Eliezer, earnestly prayed that God would direct him to the right wife for Isaac. He then joyfully thanked God for each answer he received along the way.

This reminded me of repeatedly coming down the stairs when I was a teenager and finding my mother on her knees at the living-room couch, praying out loud for her children. I would often stop and listen for when she came to my name on her list. She prayed that God would bless me and that I would dedicate my talents to the Lord, and then she always prayed for my future spouse—that God would prepare us for one another and that we would serve him together. Both her posture as she petitioned God on my behalf and the prayer itself made a profound impression on me. I'm thankful today that she lived to see those prayers answered and that she still prays for me.

On three occasions Rebekah witnessed the servant praying, and by the third time, she definitely realized that *she* was the reason he was praising God! I'm sure it influenced her regarding her choice to come to Isaac, and I'm also sure it gave her peace of mind about the tremendous changes happening in her life.

There is a deeper message than just a simple love story here. There is a great deal of symbolism in the Bible. Isaac represents a type of Christ. And Rebekah is like the church, accepting Isaac of her own free will—sight unseen. In John 20:29 Jesus said, "Blessed are those that have not seen and yet have believed."

I accepted Jesus Christ by faith when I was just five years old, and a love relationship between a little girl and a living God began that day. Sight unseen, I said "Yes," and I will never be the same. (It was a match made in heaven!) Have you accepted his proposal yet?

Everybody loves a good love story, and in case you haven't guessed, I decided to start this book with a bit of my own story and a lot of Rebekah and Isaac's story to "rope you in," hoping to give you an appetite for tasting more of what the Bible has to offer. Sure, I want you to enjoy and apply the Bible stories I'll be retelling within the pages of this book, but my *real* motive is to challenge you to start digging into God's Word for yourself.

It is my prayer that the chapters that follow will inspire and challenge you every time you pick up this book. But if I can challenge you to read the Bible for yourself, I will have accomplished a far greater purpose! I hope this book will give you a taste of the banquet that's awaiting.

> With both feet planted firmly on love, you'll be able to take in . . . the extravagant dimensions of Christ's love. Reach out and experience the breadth! Test its length! Plumb the depths! Rise to the heights! Live full lives, full in the fullness of God.
>
> Ephesians 3:17–19 Message

On the long drive home I studied Graydon's strong profile and found myself deeply contemplative. I had met him five years before and at the time would never have considered dating him, much less marrying him. We met in high school, and he was four years older than I was. He was an agnostic who loved to argue about the existence of God. I was a Christian—a minister's daughter—and a target for debate that he just couldn't pass up.

At first I was horrified by his blatant rejection of God and by his disdain of my certainty that it was possible to have a personal relationship with God by accepting, by faith, his Son, Jesus Christ. Then a deep commitment settled in my heart to pray daily for the intellectual young man who argued so forcibly, but who openly admitted to an emptiness and a lack of fulfillment in his life. Every night I earnestly prayed for my friend Graydon to come to know Christ.

Then my father accepted a pastorate about one hundred miles away, so I moved with my family. Graydon left to attend the University of Michigan, and we began corresponding two or three times a month. I wrote with a challenge: "How can you reject the Bible without reading it? You'll read anything your college professors assign to you, and you read it with an open mind. But you reject the Bible without even opening it!"

It was probably the first logical rather than emotional argument I had ever offered, and he accepted the challenge. Purchasing a Bible at the campus bookstore, he started to read. A history buff, he read the account of the creation of the world, and to my amazement, as the months went by, he chose to accept the account as historical truth. He did not, however, believe that there was any personal significance to be found within the pages of the Bible.

Three years passed, and every night a teenage girl prayed for her friend's salvation.

Then a letter arrived from Graydon, saying that he would like to make the long drive to come for a weekend, and our whole family prayed for him prior to his visit. I was filled with expectant certainty that my friend would finally choose to accept Jesus Christ. After all, as the houseguest of a pastor's family, it was expected that he would attend every service. That meant he would have three opportunities!

He came. We had both grown up, and it was wonderful to see each other again after corresponding for so long. He attended every service on Sunday but said "No" to God.

Following the evening service, Mother fixed a light supper, and she and I ate quickly and excused ourselves, abandoning Graydon to my father at the dining-room table. We quietly prayed while Dad went through most of the New Testament with him. Again Graydon said "No."

I was saddened as I said good-bye to my friend that night and frustrated with his rejection of Christ. I was worried, too. I had come across a verse of Scripture that said, "And God hardened his heart." Graydon had rejected God and ridiculed others for their beliefs more often than anyone I had ever known. Would God get sick and tired of that rejection and say, "I've had it with you, buddy. Go your own way into eternity"?

After Graydon drove away, I turned back to the house with a discouraged heart and went to my room. Standing there alone, I prayed a prayer unlike any I had ever prayed before. Reaching my arms up, I unconsciously tried to grab onto God. I clenched my fists, and with tears running down my face I cried out, "God, if I promise not to give up on him, do *you* promise not to give up on him?"

Three days later a letter with familiar writing arrived that shocked me to the core of my being. In essence, it said:

> *Dear Jennie: I was so exhausted from your father preaching to me for so long on Sunday night that I actually thought I might fall asleep at the wheel. I turned the radio on just to try to stay awake, and wouldn't you know it—I only was able to tune in to preaching programs!*

(He had tuned in to The Radio Bible Class broadcast out of Grand Rapids, Michigan, and heard an old minister by the name of M. R. DeHaan, who had a logical message for a logical listener.) His letter continued:

> *The man said, "What do you have to lose if you give your life to Christ?" Well, I thought about that, and it occurred to me that if all this was true, I had absolutely nothing to lose and everything to gain. The speaker went on to say, "Has it ever occurred to you that if you lack sufficient faith, to ask God to take what faith you have and make it enough?"*
>
> *Well, Jennie, there in my car on I-75 I started talking to God. I said, "God, I have this emptiness inside of me that nothing seems able to fill. If you're really real, will you come inside of me and fill up that void? And if you're really real, would you forgive me for all the rotten things I've said and done—especially with regard to who you are?"*

I didn't realize as I read that first testimony of my friend that years later Graydon would become my husband and the spiritual leader in our home. As we drove back from Niagara Falls the evening he proposed, I had no idea of the wonderful, challenging future that God had in store for us. It was a match made in heaven.

A Passionate Prayer

Dear Heavenly Father, thank you for the ancient love story of Isaac and Rebekah, and thank you that it has relevance to my life today. I'm so grateful that, like Rebekah, who had the right to choose Isaac, I have the choice to follow you. Please put a hunger in my heart to read and understand more of what you have for me in the Bible. Help me to read with an open mind and an open heart, and bless my honest desire to grow to know you better. I want to be like Abraham's servant, who prayed for your guidance and who was quick to thank you for answered prayer. Please give me direction and wisdom regarding the individuals in my life and the decisions that I have to make; lead me down the right road.

In Jesus's name, Amen.

The Scripture Reading: Genesis 24:1–67

Abraham was now old and well advanced in years, and the LORD had blessed him in every way. He said to the chief servant in his household, the one in charge of all that he had, "Put your hand under my thigh. I want you to swear by the LORD, the God of heaven and the God of earth, that you will not get a wife for my son from the daughters of the Canaanites, among whom I am living, but will go to my country and my own relatives and get a wife for my son Isaac."

The servant asked him, "What if the woman is unwilling to come back with me to this land? Shall I then take your son back to the country you came from?"

"Make sure that you do not take my son back there," Abraham said. "The LORD, the God of heaven, who brought me out of my father's household and my native land and who spoke to me and promised me on oath, saying, 'To your offspring I will give this land'—he will send his angel before you so that you can get a wife for my son from there. If the woman is unwilling to come back with you, then you will be released from this oath of mine. Only do not take my son back there." So the servant put his hand under the thigh of his master Abraham and swore an oath to him concerning this matter.

Then the servant took ten of his master's camels and left, taking with him all kinds of good things from his master. He set out for Aram Naharaim and made his way to the town of Nahor. He had the camels kneel down near the well outside the town; it was toward evening, the time the women go out to draw water.

Then he prayed, "O LORD, God of my master Abraham, give me success today, and show kindness to my master Abraham. See, I am standing beside this spring, and the daughters of the townspeople are coming out to draw water. May it be that when I say to a girl, 'Please let down your jar that I may have a drink,' and she says, 'Drink, and I'll water your camels too'—let her be the one you have chosen for your servant Isaac. By this I will know that you have shown kindness to my master."

Before he had finished praying, Rebekah came out with her jar on her shoulder. She was the daughter of Bethuel son of Milcah, who was the wife of Abraham's brother Nahor. The girl was very beautiful, a virgin; no man had ever lain with her. She went down to the spring, filled her jar and came up again.

The servant hurried to meet her and said, "Please give me a little water from your jar."

"Drink, my lord," she said, and quickly lowered the jar to her hands and gave him a drink.

After she had given him a drink, she said, "I'll draw water for your camels too, until they have finished drinking." So she quickly emptied her jar into the trough, ran back to the well to draw more water, and drew enough for all his camels. Without saying a word, the man watched her closely to learn whether or not the LORD had made his journey successful.

When the camels had finished drinking, the man took out a gold nose ring weighing a beka and two gold bracelets weighing ten shekels. Then he asked, "Whose daughter are you? Please tell me, is there room in your father's house for us to spend the night?"

She answered him, "I am the daughter of Bethuel, the son that Milcah bore to Nahor." And she added, "We have plenty of straw and fodder, as well as a room for you to spend the night."

Then the man bowed down and worshiped the LORD, saying, "Praise be to the LORD, the God of my master Abraham, who has not abandoned his kindness and faithfulness to my master. As for me, the LORD has led me on the journey to the house of my master's relatives."

The girl ran and told her mother's household about these things. Now Rebekah had a brother named Laban, and he hurried out to the man at the spring. As soon as he had seen the nose ring, and the bracelets on his sister's arms, and had heard Rebekah tell what the man said to her, he went out to the man and found him standing by the camels near the spring. "Come, you who are blessed by the LORD," he said. "Why are you standing out here? I have prepared the house and a place for the camels."

So the man went to the house, and the camels were unloaded. Straw and fodder were brought for the camels, and water for him and his men to wash their feet. Then food was set before him, but he said, "I will not eat until I have told you what I have to say."

"Then tell us," Laban said.

So he said, "I am Abraham's servant. The LORD has blessed my master abundantly, and he has become wealthy. He has given him sheep and cattle, silver and gold, menservants and maidservants, and camels and donkeys. My master's wife Sarah has borne him a son in her old age, and he has given him everything he owns. And my master made me swear an oath, and said, 'You must not get a wife for my son from the daughters of the Canaanites, in whose land I live, but go to my father's family and to my own clan, and get a wife for my son.'

"Then I asked my master, 'What if the woman will not come back with me?'

"He replied, 'The LORD, before whom I have walked, will send his angel with you and make your journey a success, so that you can get a wife for my son from my own clan and from my father's family. Then, when you go to my clan, you will be released from my oath even if they refuse to give her to you—you will be released from my oath.'

"When I came to the spring today, I said, 'O LORD, God of my master Abraham, if you will, please grant success to the journey on which I have come. See, I am standing beside this spring; if a maiden comes out to draw water and I say to her, "Please let me drink a little water from your jar," and if she says to me, "Drink, and

I'll draw water for your camels too," let her be the one the LORD has chosen for my master's son.'

"Before I finished praying in my heart, Rebekah came out, with her jar on her shoulder. She went down to the spring and drew water, and I said to her, 'Please give me a drink.'

"She quickly lowered her jar from her shoulder and said, 'Drink, and I'll water your camels too.' So I drank, and she watered the camels also.

"I asked her, 'Whose daughter are you?'

"She said, 'The daughter of Bethuel son of Nahor, whom Milcah bore to him.'

"Then I put the ring in her nose and the bracelets on her arms, and I bowed down and worshiped the LORD. I praised the LORD, the God of my master Abraham, who had led me on the right road to get the granddaughter of my master's brother for his son. Now if you will show kindness and faithfulness to my master, tell me; and if not, tell me, so I may know which way to turn."

Laban and Bethuel answered, "This is from the LORD; we can say nothing to you one way or the other. Here is Rebekah; take her and go, and let her become the wife of your master's son, as the LORD has directed."

When Abraham's servant heard what they said, he bowed down to the ground before the LORD. Then the servant brought out gold and silver jewelry and articles of clothing and gave them to Rebekah; he also gave costly gifts to her brother and to her mother. Then he and the men who were with him ate and drank and spent the night there.

When they got up the next morning, he said, "Send me on my way to my master."

But her brother and her mother replied, "Let the girl remain with us ten days or so; then you may go."

But he said to them, "Do not detain me, now that the LORD has granted success to my journey. Send me on my way so I may go to my master."

Then they said, "Let's call the girl and ask her about it." So they called Rebekah and asked her, "Will you go with this man?"

"I will go," she said.

So they sent their sister Rebekah on her way, along with her nurse and Abraham's servant and his men. And they blessed Rebekah and said to her,

> "Our sister, may you increase to thousands upon thousands; may your offspring possess the gates of their enemies."

Then Rebekah and her maids got ready and mounted their camels and went back with the man. So the servant took Rebekah and left.

Now Isaac had come from Beer Lahai Roi, for he was living in the Negev. He went out to the field one evening to meditate, and as he looked up, he saw camels approaching. Rebekah also looked up and saw Isaac. She got down from her camel and asked the servant, "Who is that man in the field coming to meet us?"

"He is my master," the servant answered. So she took her veil and covered herself.

Then the servant told Isaac all he had done. Isaac brought her into the tent of his mother Sarah, and he married Rebekah. So she became his wife, and he loved her; and Isaac was comforted after his mother's death.

Final Note: The story of Isaac and Rebekah was recorded during the fifth century, BC. Read Genesis 22–35 for a more complete understanding of Isaac's birth and childhood, as well as of the twins born to Isaac and Rebekah later in their marriage and the complex relationships that developed within their extended family. (These additional chapters also give Eliezer's name and refer to Rebekah's nursemaid, Deborah.)

2

Choosing to Trust
A Story about Daring Faith

Susie could hardly contain her excitement! During show-and-tell she made the big announcement to her kindergarten class: "We're going to have a new baby at our house!"

The class was delighted for her, but every time they had show-and-tell, Susie's contribution was just one more variation of the same announcement: "We're getting a new baby!"

One day when she came home from school, her mother excitedly motioned for Susie with one hand while holding her protruding abdomen with the other.

"Come here right now, honey. Put your hands on Mama's tummy, and you'll feel the baby move!"

Susie was shocked! She slowly walked forward, placed both of her hands on her mother's stomach, but, although her eyes got huge in her face, didn't say a word.

The following day, the class dutifully waited for Susie's regular announcement. But she didn't say a word. The next day came, and the next. Nothing. A whole week went by. The teacher became concerned. Susie had been so excited about that baby for so long and was now so silent that the teacher wondered if Susie's mother had miscarried. She waited until nap time, when the other children were resting, and then called Susie up to her desk. Placing an arm gently around the child's shoulders, she asked, "Susie, are you still going to have a new baby at your house?"

Susie seemed distressed. She wrung her little hands and, sighing, she looked up. "I'm not sure, Teacher," she confided. "Cuz, you see, I think my mommy *ate* it!"[1]

Oh my! With such a misconception, no wonder Susie was distressed! On the heels of that baby story, I want to tell you a story that's not so funny, a story about another little girl whose mom was expecting a baby. This story is recorded in Exodus 1 and 2, and it is the story of a family who chose to trust God during a time of great despair.

Jochebed's Story

"Ahhhh, yes. Thank you, Miriam. I've been longing for this."

Jochebed straightened to accept the cup of water her daughter handed her, wearily reaching back with her other hand to rub her aching spine.

"Are you all right, Mother?" Miriam asked quietly.

Glancing furtively to her left, Jochebed saw a taskmaster roughly shove aside an elderly man burdened with an armload of hay for the brick makers. The old man stumbled, almost managing to keep his balance before losing the struggle and collapsing against another laborer. Hay spewed everywhere. The taskmaster raised his whip.

"Go on and bring refreshment to the others," said Jochebed, hastily steering the little girl away from the distressing scene and out of the taskmaster's path. "I'm fine, Miriam. I'm fine. I'll see you tonight."

Miriam made eye contact with her mother for a moment, then picked up the water jug and moved quietly on her way.

"Oh, Lord, how long?" prayed Jochebed as she bent once again to her task. "How long?"

It was after sundown when the signal finally came. Jochebed wearily nodded to several other exhausted laborers and turned away. She made her way to the river, gingerly picking her way through the tall grass, carefully watching for crocodiles. She sank down on the bank and immersed her swollen feet and ankles in the cool water of the Nile. Her sigh of relief was audible, yet her heart ached silently. Under her full garment her body was swollen with child. How much longer could she keep her family's secret?

The Israelites had lived in the land of Egypt since the days of Joseph and the great famine that brought them there. In Egypt they had prospered and multiplied. But as the generations passed, a king arose who saw the many children of Israel as both a threat and an opportunity to enhance his kingdom. He enslaved the people and launched a huge architectural campaign to build two treasure cities. Working the Hebrews ruthlessly, he hoped to weaken the strong ones and kill off the weak ones, while at the same time building elaborate cities for storage and for showcasing the wealth of Egypt.

The first plan failed. Instead of growing weaker, the Israelites grew stronger and continued to multiply.

So Pharaoh changed his tactic. He called in the Hebrew midwives and mandated that they put to death every male child they delivered.

This second plan failed. The Hebrew midwives feared God more than they feared the king of Egypt. They disobeyed Pharaoh and saved the baby boys, so Pharaoh decreed that his people were to raid the vast Hebrew slave community, take the male infants by force, and drown them in the Nile.

It was during this time that Jochebed found herself pregnant with her third child.

Only one small lamp lit the humble scene of birth. Overwhelmed with pain, Jochebed stifled her cry and pushed again, desperately trying to expel the infant from her womb. Amram, standing guard at the door of their quarters, gave a furtive look of caution to the midwife, fearing that soldiers patrolling the vast slave community would hear his wife and burst in upon them. Little Miriam, her eyes wide with both fear and wonder and her cheeks streaked with tears, gently wiped the sweat from her mother's face and neck.

A deep-throated groan escaped from the depths of Jochebed's soul as she gave the final push that thrust her child into the world. It was over. Her head fell back in relief, but even through the fog of pain her mind strained for the announcement. She felt the weight of the infant as it was laid across her belly and heard the midwife move the birthing stool to attend to the afterbirth. Straining to see the child, Jochebed reached down a hand and touched a dark, sticky head. Her eyes met those of the midwife.

"It's a boy," the woman said soberly.

Jochebed's eyes flew to Amram, and the intensity of the look they exchanged spoke volumes.

"A son," she whispered, and a tear trickled down her face as joy and sorrow comingled within her.

The baby was wrapped and laid against her breast. Amram dared to leave his post at the door to kneel beside his wife and child, encircling them both in his arms. His pride and joy at the birth of his son were frustrated by the reality of the danger that now threatened them. They had not received an easy answer to their prayers.

"He's beautiful, Amram," whispered Jochebed. "So beautiful."

Her eyes drifted shut with utter exhaustion. She spoke just a few more words before sleep claimed her. "But, Amram, God gave us a boy. He gave us a boy."

They did not choose to obey the king. They hid their son for three months.

The following weeks and months were fraught with tension for Jochebed. She was a working mother with a hungry infant to feed and hide from Pharaoh's soldiers. Little Miriam's help was invaluable, but the baby was getting bigger and louder. There had been too many close calls. It was only a matter of time before the soldiers patrolling the vast slave community pounded on the entrance to their quarters, yelling, "Is there an infant here? We were not aware there was an infant in the household of Amram!"

So far God had protected the child, but how long could she go on like this? Jochebed had exhausted every resource she could think of. Then, when she could hide the baby no longer, God gave her an idea that would place the child at the very location where the other baby boys had died. The Nile River.

Jochebed wove the large basket tightly, pulling the strips of papyrus in and out. She stirred a batch of tar and pitch over the fire, and, taking a stick, daubed the basket over and over, smearing the gooey substance across the surface. It certainly wasn't the loveliest basket she'd ever made, but it was sturdy and watertight. And it would carry precious cargo.

Well aware that she was about to plunge two young children into a life-and-death situation, she went over and over the important responsibility Miriam would undertake as the drama unfolded. Her mind raced, considering the different variables that might occur. What if the soldiers saw them? What if the basket started drifting downstream? What if the crocodiles came? What if everything went according to their plan and the princess came down to the river to bathe? How should little Miriam approach this royal person? Should she curtsy or bow to the ground? What words should come out of her mouth? Jochebed sighed as she considered these things, but her resolve was sure. By faith, she chose to trust God with her children.

Jochebed arose in the darkness and gathered her baby in her arms to nurse him for what might be the last time. She memorized the silken feel of his skin and the shape of his tiny toes and feet. Tucking him in the basket, she woke Miriam and fed her a hasty breakfast. Then, with the basket resting on her hip, she stepped out into the darkness with Miriam.

"Come quickly, and be as quiet as you can," she whispered. "We mustn't be seen."

Jochebed sniffed the air. She had watched the sunset last night, and from that and the smell of the air this morning, she thought the weather would be right. Perhaps the princess would come to her spot on the river to bathe and refresh herself today. Jochebed prayed it would be so.

The grass was damp on Jochebed's feet, and she could hear the sounds of the river as they came closer. Reaching the embankment, she knelt and gathered the baby in her arms, burping him one last time, feeling his baby softness against her neck, inhaling the milky fragrance of his breath.

Jochebed tucked him into the basket, covering him carefully so no bugs could crawl on him. Then she gathered the hem of her skirt into her waistband, lifted the basket back up to her hip, and, with Miriam watching her every move, stepped into the cool morning water of the Nile. She waded out to where the bulrushes were thick, a spot where she didn't think the basket would drift away. Then she let go. She let go and let God do what he would.

Jochebed turned and moved almost silently back through the water toward the shore where Miriam was crouched. Mindless of her sodden skirts, she knelt down and reached to hold the child's shoulders. So much would now depend on a young girl. A young girl and an almighty God.

"Watch carefully, Miriam, and be as quiet as you can. Remember everything we talked about. Remember how to approach the princess and what to say. I must go, before we are found out. Oh, don't be afraid, Miriam. You are not alone. God is with you."

It was a hot and hazy day, and the princess instructed her maidens to accompany her to the river to bathe. Much cooler there, they relaxed and lingered, finding it refreshing to stroll up and down the riverbank. Pharaoh's daughter was smiling in response to the chatter of her attendants when she heard a small cry. Shading her eyes with her hand, she scanned the river.

"Did you hear that?" she asked the others. "I thought I heard a baby cry."

The small cry became a wail, and her eyes landed on an odd basketlike craft nestled in the bulrushes a short distance beyond her bathing area.

"Look! Over there! Fetch it for me!"

Wading into the marshy area, the maidens retrieved the basket, which was resounding with the hungry cry of a baby, and delivered it to their mistress. She lifted the covering carefully and stared with wonder at the contents.

She expected to see a baby after hearing the impatient cry. What she was not prepared for, however, was the jolt of longing that overwhelmed her at the sight of the beautiful infant. She fingered the plain, coarse swaddling cloth.

"This is a Hebrew child," she said while reaching to take the baby from the basket. "A very wet male child!" she laughed, lifting him out of the wet strips of cloth.

To the amazement of her attendants, she enfolded him in her arms, with little regard for her costly garment. Consoled for just a moment, the baby nuzzled against her and then started fussing in frustration.

"And he's more than a little hungry, I would guess," she chuckled.

"Oh, Princess!"

A small voice called out from the tall grass, and Pharaoh's daughter looked up to see a young Hebrew girl. The girl's eyes were wide with nervousness, but she bravely approached the royal party. After making a curtsy of sorts, and while wringing her small hands together, she offered, "Would you like me to find a Hebrew woman to nurse the baby for you?"

"Yes, child. I would like that very much!" laughed the princess. "And hurry!"

"Yes, ma'am!" The girl bobbed another curtsy and turned to race off in the direction she had come.

"What will you do with him, Mistress?" asked one of the maidens. "It looks like some Hebrew has been disobeying your father's orders."

41

"Do with him?" The princess looked up at her attendants for a few seconds before lowering her face to brush her nose against the baby's soft head. "He is to be my *son*."

The hours seemed to drag by like years for Jochebed as she toiled that morning. Her every thought was on the unseen drama unfolding at the river. She swallowed her anxiety and, through faith, sought peace instead. God was in control.

Then in the distance she heard Miriam calling to her!

"Mama! Mama! The princess came!" In Miriam's excitement, the words tumbled over each other. "I remembered what to say, Mama! Oh, come quickly! I think we're going to get our baby back!"

An overwhelming rush of relief washed over Jochebed, and tears stung her eyes.

"Oh, Lord God, Jehovah, thank you!" Jochebed raised her face toward heaven, crying out her thanksgiving before turning to Miriam. "Come, my daughter, let's go get our baby back!"

Jochebed and Miriam hurried back to the river. Just before presenting themselves, Jochebed paused to smooth her hair and straighten her clothing. She had bound her breasts that day, but her discomfort was increasing by the moment. She could hear her child crying in the distance, and her heart raced with nervous tension. Stepping out into the clearing by the river, Jochebed presented herself humbly before the powerful woman who held her child.

"Your Highness. My daughter tells me you require a nurse for your child. I have recently lost my son, as have many of my Hebrew sisters. My breasts are full. I would be pleased to care for this child for you."

Daring to raise her eyes to Pharaoh's daughter's face, Jochebed found her eyes held by the other woman's for a moment. Then the princess held out the squalling baby to her and said, "Take this child away and nurse him for me. Care for him well, and I will pay you wages."

Speechless at the news and choked with emotion, Jochebed reached out with trembling hands to take the child into her arms.

"His name will be Moses," said the Princess, "because I drew him from the water."

Joy sang in Jochebed's and Miriam's hearts as they left with the child. God had honored their faith and saved the baby's life! In addition, Jochebed was raised from the position of slave to the position of wet nurse and nanny to little Prince Moses, who was to become Pharaoh's grandson. But she would concern herself with that detail another day. Her babe was in her arms once again!

Jochebed went home to share the astounding news with Amram, not realizing that God would one day use her little son to answer her prayer for the freedom of her people.

Digging Deeper

The story of Jochebed and her family is a story of enduring faith in the face of impossible circumstances and a story of God's amazing provision. As we look more deeply into the life and times of this family, there is a remarkable message of hope for each of us today. Take a closer look at the story with me.

What is the setting of this story? If you're curious about how the Israelites came to live in Egypt in the first place, you need to look back almost four hundred years prior to the story of Jochebed and read about Joseph (Genesis 37–Exodus 2). In a nutshell, Joseph, the son of Jacob (and grandson of Isaac from the previous chapter), became an important man in both Hebrew and Egyptian history. Although he had been sold into Egyptian slavery in his youth, he was later revered for warning the Egyptian ruler that a seven-year famine would come after seven years of plenty and for advising that food should be stored for the future. When these predictions proved true, Pharaoh elevated Joseph to the position of governor of the land, second only to Pharaoh himself. Later, when Joseph's brothers made the trek into Egypt during the famine to purchase grain, Joseph was reunited with part of his clan. Pharaoh then invited Joseph's entire family to relocate with their flocks to the fertile area of Goshen. So the first Hebrews made their way into the land of Egypt. Those relatives, numbering about seventy persons in all, were honored and respected (Genesis 45:16–20) and came to prosper and multiply in the land. (Joseph and his eleven brothers were the fathers of the twelve tribes of Israel, which eventually grew to a population of well over two million people.)

Then things changed. After about three hundred years, a new dynasty came to power. Its pharaohs did not acknowledge Joseph or credit his efforts to save Egypt, and the Israelites were enslaved. As our story opens, Jochebed and her family are part of a vast slave population that has been exploited by a cruel monarch. As years of abuse continued, the Goshen area became a ghetto, and life was a bitter existence.

Then came Pharaoh's cruel edict. Pharaoh's first two attempts to thin out the Hebrew population failed, so the ruler decreed that the male babies should be thrown in the Nile River. It is the first reference in Scripture to infanticide.

Several years ago I heard Charles Swindoll speak on his radio program about this story. He made a sober comment that was so graphic I will never forget it: "Imagine how the crocodiles thrived on the Nile River the year they feasted on baby boys."

These were real people, living during a heartbreaking time in history. And in the middle of these bitterly difficult times, a woman named Jochebed got pregnant for the third time.

Have *you* ever questioned God's timing in your life? I'm afraid I have. I've also wondered if Jochebed and Amram prayed for a girl. Although great value was placed on the number of sons a man had, a girl certainly would have been an easy answer to a terrifying problem! Instead, the birth of their son tested their faith, and they rose to the challenge, defying Pharaoh by hiding their son from the hand of death.

How did they dare? Amram and Jochebed were from the tribe of Levi, which was the tribe that priests were chosen from. They had a godly heritage. It had been prophesied in the book of Genesis that the Israelites would be enslaved but that the fourth generation would be set free (Genesis 15:13–16). Times were terrible, but they remembered God's promise.

God worked miracles in Jochebed's life.

The princess decided to make the infant her own son.
Amazing. Whose daughter was she? *Pharaoh's.* What kind
of prejudice was there against the Hebrew people in the
land? *Overwhelming.* That powerful woman could have had
her pick of the most beautiful Egyptian boy babies in all
the land, but God put a desire in her heart to adopt a child
from another race, a race that was being oppressed by her
own father. She would bring the child into Pharaoh's own
household, where he would grow up with the status of a
royal grandson and receive the finest education.

**God so honored Jochebed's faith that he saw to it that
the princess hired Jochebed to nurse and care for the
child.** We're not told whether Pharaoh's daughter ever
suspected that Jochebed had borne the child, but we do
know that she had no intention of allowing Jochebed
to keep the baby. She wanted him for herself. But not
only was Jochebed allowed to care for the child, she was
elevated from the status of slave to a paid employee of
the royal family.

**Amram and Jochebed chose to trust God with their impos-
sible situation, and God took away their fear.** Hebrews
11:23, in the famous "heroes of the faith" chapter of the
Bible, says, "By faith Moses' parents hid him for three
months after he was born, because they saw he was no
ordinary child, *and they were not afraid* of the king's edict"
(italics added).

Amram and Jochebed not only had to trust God to preserve
their baby's life, they had to trust him when the time came to give
the baby up to the home of their enemy. It is interesting to note
that Jochebed must have used her time as nanny to teach the
little prince to honor God. This is what the Bible says about how
he turned out: "By faith Moses, when he had grown up, refused
to be known as the son of Pharaoh's daughter. He chose to be

45

mistreated along with the people of God rather than to enjoy the pleasures of sin for a short time" (Hebrews 11:24–25). He eventually led the Israelites out of bondage.

How can this story apply to your life?

What is your impossible situation today? Is it financial? Is it a wayward child, an impossible job situation, or a marital problem? Terminally ill parents, or the loss of a loved one?

I want to remind you that the same God who loved Jochebed and had a plan for her life and for her family loves you and has a special plan for your life as well. In Jeremiah 29:11–13 there is an awesome promise to remember: "'For I know the plans I have for you,' declares the LORD, 'plans to prosper you and not to harm you, plans to give you hope and a future. Then you will call upon me and come and pray to me, and I will listen to you. You will seek me and find me when you seek me with all your heart.'"

Will you choose to trust God with your situation? Picture a big ugly basket covered with tar and pitch. Now think of that burden that wakes you up in the middle of the night and robs you of precious peace of mind. Can you, by faith, put your burden in the basket? By faith, step into the water and let go of the basket, trusting that God will work this out for good in your life?

Choose to trust him. It can make *all* the difference.

John Sr. bent down to hoist pajama-clad, four-year-old John Jr. up in his arms and headed for the stairs. He made sure that Johnny brushed his teeth and got one last drink of water, then raced the little boy to his bedroom. They both knew the ritual. John Sr. would tuck Johnny into bed and read him a Bible story; then Johnny would say his prayers, wait for the warmth of his dad's goodnight kiss on his forehead, and snuggle under the covers while his dad said a final "Goodnight, son" as he turned off the light on his way out of the room.

Downstairs again, John Sr. helped himself to some orange juice from the fridge. Before heading for his recliner, he bent to kiss his wife on the cheek as she concentrated on balancing their checkbook at the kitchen table. Then he headed for the living room, positioned his drink on the end table, and settled into his chair with the remote control in one hand and his newspaper in the other. His sigh of contentment was audible.

He was just turning to the first page of the sports section when he heard a familiar small voice calling from the top of the stairs.

"Daddy? I'm afraid of the dark."

Not again, John thought with a little irritation. Lowering his paper but not bothering to get up, he called to his son.

"Go back to bed, Johnny. You're not alone. God is with you. Now go back to bed, son."

So Johnny padded back to bed.

Just a few minutes passed, then the same small voice called down again.

"Daddy? Will you send Mom up here, and I'll send God down there? I think I need somebody with skin on 'em."[2]

I find myself laughing at Johnny, but the truth is, I've been just like him on many occasions. When I'm afraid, or feel helpless, or can't bear to face the challenges ahead of me, what do I do? Oh, I call my mom, or my husband at work, or my sister, or my neighbor, because I know that all those people love me and will help, encourage, or pray for me. What I forget while I'm so busy rushing around contacting people with "skin on 'em" is that I have a powerful God who loves me, who has an awesome plan he wants to work out in my life, and who is just waiting for me to remember to call upon him.

A Passionate Prayer

Dear Heavenly Father, I need your help. I'm so tired of trying to manage my life and difficult situations in my own strength. Right now, I'm choosing to trust you. Help me to let go and to quit trying

*to manipulate things to work out the way I think is best. Thank you
for loving me and for caring about my problems.*
Please take away my fear like you did for Jochebed and Amram.
*Exchange my anxiety for your peace. Help me to rest in the
knowledge that you have a special plan for my life.*
In the precious name of Jesus, Amen.

The Scripture Reading: Exodus 1:6–2:10

Now Joseph and all his brothers and all that generation died, but
the Israelites were fruitful and multiplied greatly and became
exceedingly numerous, so that the land was filled with them.

Then a new king, who did not know about Joseph, came to power
in Egypt. "Look," he said to his people, "the Israelites have become
much too numerous for us. Come, we must deal shrewdly with them
or they will become even more numerous and, if war breaks out, will
join our enemies, fight against us and leave the country."

So they put slave masters over them to oppress them with forced
labor, and they built Pithom and Rameses as store cities for Pharaoh.
But the more they were oppressed, the more they multiplied and
spread; so the Egyptians came to dread the Israelites and worked
them ruthlessly. They made their lives bitter with hard labor in brick
and mortar and with all kinds of work in the fields; in all their hard
labor the Egyptians used them ruthlessly.

The king of Egypt said to the Hebrew midwives, whose names
were Shiphrah and Puah, "When you help the Hebrew women in
childbirth and observe them on the delivery stool, if it is a boy, kill
him; but if it is a girl, let her live." The midwives, however, feared
God and did not do what the king of Egypt had told them to do;
they let the boys live. Then the king of Egypt summoned the
midwives and asked them, "Why have you done this? Why have you
let the boys live?"

The midwives answered Pharaoh, "Hebrew women are not like
Egyptian women; they are vigorous and give birth before the
midwives arrive."

So God was kind to the midwives and the people increased and
became even more numerous. And because the midwives feared
God, he gave them families of their own.

Then Pharaoh gave this order to all his people: "Every boy that is born you must throw into the river, but let every girl live."

Now a man of the house of Levi married a Levite woman, and she became pregnant and gave birth to a son. When she saw that he was a fine child, she hid him for three months. But when she could hide him no longer, she got a papyrus basket for him and coated it with tar and pitch. Then she placed the child in it and put it among the reeds along the bank of the Nile. His sister stood at a distance to see what would happen to him.

Then Pharaoh's daughter went down to the Nile to bathe, and her attendants were walking along the river bank. She saw the basket among the reeds and sent her slave girl to get it. She opened it and saw the baby. He was crying, and she felt sorry for him. "This is one of the Hebrew babies," she said.

Then his sister asked Pharaoh's daughter, "Shall I go and get one of the Hebrew women to nurse the baby for you?"

"Yes, go," she answered. And the girl went and got the baby's mother. Pharaoh's daughter said to her, "Take this baby and nurse him for me, and I will pay you." So the woman took the baby and nursed him. When the child grew older, she took him to Pharaoh's daughter and he became her son. She named him Moses, saying, "I drew him out of the water."

Final Note: The Book of Exodus records the birth of the nation of Israel, their bitter servitude to the Egyptians, and their deliverance from Egypt, led by Moses, the son of Amram and Jochebed. It was recorded in approximately 1450–1405 BC.

3

Me First, Me First!
A Story for Leaders

Pastor Mike Hollenbeck and his wife, Joyce, were married for seventeen years without children. Then they adopted two beautiful daughters. They came to visit us for a few days when their daughter Kacie was a five-year-old and their daughter Jordyn was an infant, and the joy that our dear friends exhibited over their growing family was a delight for our own family to witness.

Kacie was a winsome, precocious child with red hair and a little body that was covered with freckles. Joyce confided to me on the second day of their visit that, for all her good points, Kacie was quite a handful.

"She's going through this stage where she wants to be the *boss* of everything and everyone," Joyce said, shaking her head. "She puts her little hands on her hips and announces that she's the boss of her room, the boss of her toys, and the boss of her baby sister. Her nursery school teacher says she tries to be the boss there, too!"

The following evening I was rinsing some dishes in the kitchen sink when Kacie walked in and sweetly asked me for three pieces of fudge from the plate on the counter. Turning to look at her, I responded, "I don't think so, honey, but if it's okay with your mommy, I'd be happy to give you one piece."

Moments later she returned with the required permission, and I handed her the promised treat on a napkin. After taking her first bite, she cocked her little head at me and said with a mischievous grin, "Aunt Jennie, I was just fooling you when I asked for three."

Nodding, I chuckled and started to turn back to the sink, only to be arrested by her next announcement. With one hand holding the fudge and the other placed importantly on her hip, she said thoughtfully, "You're not my boss, but when your daddy's gone, you're the boss at this house, aren't you?"

I laughed out loud, and as I got on with my work, I smiled, thinking, "At least Mike and Joyce's challenge comes packaged with a lot of humor!"

Three days after their visit ended, a note came in the mail.

Dear Graydon and Jennie,

Thanks a lot for the wonderful visit in Fremont. We had a great trip home with the kids sleeping most of the way. On Monday, Kacie approached Mike about accepting Jesus as her Savior, and when she prayed, she asked God to come in and to be the "Boss" of her life. She really seems different, Jennie. Why is it that I expect God to work powerfully in the lives of adults, but I forget that he can change a child's life just as beautifully? Anyway, we are rejoicing.

Thanks again for the fun, food, and fellowship.

Love, Joyce

I've thought about that letter many times in the years since it arrived, and I have had the opportunity to observe Kacie grow from a little girl into a remarkable teenager with tremendous enthusiasm and the ability to win others to Christ. What happened to the bossy little girl that was filled with her own importance? Well, she not only asked Jesus into her heart, but she also asked him to be her *Boss*—her Lord. She put him first in her life. And it made all the difference.

There is a rather haunting story in the Old Testament about a gifted and talented woman, once a charming child and mightily used of God, who made the mistake of trying to be the boss. You'll recognize her as the story progresses, and in it there's an important lesson for each of us.

Miriam's Story

Unclean. For the hundredth time the old woman stared down at her hands and shuddered . . . remembering. Shame engulfed her as she recalled her foolish arrogance, her willful pride, her reckless tongue. How could she have strayed so far when she, of all people, should have known better?

It was quiet here where she was confined outside the camp. She had been terrified the first night she'd been separated from the warm laughter around the campfires—she had never been so alone, so separated from the fellowship of the families who made up the vast company of the children of Israel. Twelve tribes in all, with flags flying for each, they were indeed a sight to behold. How amazing that she, Miriam, had been one of their esteemed leaders. She snorted in self-derision.

If only she could turn back time. She longed to take back her brash arrogance, her prejudice, her sin against her brother, her sister-in-law, and her Lord. How had she strayed so far from a right relationship with God? She stopped swaying and stared across the expanse of land before her, while in her mind's eye she focused on years past.

The years of slavery had been grueling, unforgettable. Abuse, fear, death, bitterness. Miriam had witnessed it all. She marveled at the strength of her mother, Jochebed, her unwavering faith during her last pregnancy, and her refusal to abide by the edict of Pharaoh.

Miriam's thoughts flickered to the clandestine trek she and her mother had made to the river's edge to hide the baby among the bulrushes. She could almost smell the river and seemed to be once again peering through the tall grass. Her heart pounded as she remembered how alone she felt when Jochebed left her to watch over the baby. But she had not been alone. God had been with her.

Pharaoh's daughter had come to the edge of the Nile to bathe. A cry pierced the air, and Miriam froze as she watched the princess look up and notice the homely ark floating among the rushes.

"Please, God, please help us!" Miriam's young heart cried when she witnessed the elegant woman lifting the wet and hungry baby out of the basket. Trembling, she approached the powerful woman and asked if she would like her to fetch a nurse for the baby. She then raced to get her mother. Jochebed was elevated from a lowly slave to the position of paid wet nurse and nanny for the baby, who was to become the son of Pharaoh's daughter herself! The day that had started with such fear and tension had ended in jubilation.

Miriam paused to heave a sigh at the recollection of events that seemed so real but had happened over eighty years ago. Shaking her head, she sighed again.

The years following that day by the Nile River were difficult for the Hebrews, but, in spite of the hardships, Miriam was bathed in the faith of her family and the Levite tribe. Growing up in that godly tribe, she not only was aware of God's laws and promises, but in witnessing God's provision for her little brother, she also saw glimpses of life beyond the misery of the slave compound. Somehow God would deliver them, but how? When? Would he use baby Moses? Would he use her?

After Moses went to live with the princess, Miriam rarely saw him, and for the next forty years Pharaoh was relentless in his abuse of the Hebrew people. Occasionally Miriam or Aaron, her other brother, caught a glimpse of Moses in the distance, standing from some elevated position, watching the massive construction projects taking place. He had grown to manhood, and his dress and manner were Egyptian. Did he recall his heritage at all? Would he one day help to free his people?

Then a royal scandal occurred, and the news spread like wildfire through the slave camp. Prince Moses had witnessed an Egyptian overseer brutally beating a slave and had killed the Egyptian! When Pharaoh heard the news, he was so furious he ordered that Moses be put to death.

And Moses ran for his life.

Miriam wearily closed her eyes, remembering the conflicting emotions she had experienced. At first she was fiercely proud that Moses had stood up and defended one of his own people. Then she was so afraid he would be caught, and then relieved to hear that he had escaped. But with his departure and in the long years that followed, there had been such temptation to wallow in despair. God had promised their forefather, Abraham, that they would be set free, but how? When would deliverance come?

Forty more bitter years dragged by, and the children of Israel cried out to God for deliverance. Then God sent their deliverer, and it was Moses.

He came back! Almost unrecognizable from the groomed and fashionable Egyptian he had once been, Moses appeared bearded and weathered by the sun and wind. His forty years in the land of Midian had been spent shepherding. He had married the daughter of a priest. He earnestly told the Israelites of an astounding encounter with God, who showed himself in a burning bush. And despite his impressive Egyptian education, he was a humble man. He struggled with speaking publicly, and yet he had a God-given boldness to go before Pharaoh and demand freedom for the Israelites.

Hope burned once again in Miriam's heart! Their brother Aaron stood with Moses and often was his spokesman, but it was Moses whom God empowered to do truly miraculous things. As Moses stood before Pharaoh, his staff became a snake! Then, when he picked it up by the tail, it became a staff again! He touched the Nile and it turned to blood. Frogs came from nowhere and were everywhere! Hail beat down upon Egypt, and then swarms of locusts came and ate everything that was left. In spite of pestilence, plagues, and darkness, Pharaoh refused to let the people go, until the night of death: Passover.

Moses warned Pharaoh that if he did not release the Israelites, the firstborn in every household would die. The Israelites were told that to escape this death they should prepare bread without yeast and slay and roast a lamb, brushing its blood over the side and upper doorposts of their homes.

But Pharaoh refused to believe. At midnight, death came. Grief overwhelmed the land of Egypt, and no unmarked house escaped the wrath of God. With the death of his son, his heir, Pharaoh finally gave up his hold on the Israelites; he implored them to go and to take herds of cattle and other livestock with them.

Miriam's face creased in a weathered smile as she remembered their triumphant exodus. What a sight! Over two million people left Egypt. There were six hundred thousand men, plus the women and children, and three people led them: Moses, Aaron, and Miriam, with the presence of God before them day and night.

The challenges of the exodus were many, but looking back, Miriam could see how God sought to use each challenge to teach and to reveal himself to his people. The first obstacle came when they reached the sea. Pharaoh had changed his mind and wanted the Israelites back as slaves, so he sent his vast army, including horsemen and officers with six hundred chariots to pursue them. The people were trapped. Terrified. But God spoke to Moses, and Moses lifted his staff over the water.

A fierce wind blew, the water divided sharply to the left and to the right, and amazingly, dry ground lay ahead of them. It was no small task to get that many people through such a strange and terrifying passageway, but the strong helped those crippled by age and abuse. Twelve tribes of men, women, children, and the livestock they had taken with them crossed the sea. Some pulled carts. Everyone carried burdens.

"Hurry, people. Hurry! Pharaoh's troops are just behind us!"

But where were the Egyptians? Miriam and the others soon realized that God had positioned his own presence in the form of a pillar of cloud between his people and their enemy. He caused the darkness of night to face the Egyptians but gave light for the Israelites to find their way.

All that night, the arduous exodus continued. In the morning, when the people were safely on the opposite shore, God lifted the cloud behind them and the Israelites witnessed the Egyptian army charging through that same hollow cavity. Suddenly, God caused the wheels to fall off the chariots, creating confusion and an effective roadblock. The soldiers behind the chariots kept coming. Then when the entire army had entered the sea floor, God told Moses to again stretch out his staff over the water.

The cry of the people on shore and the terrified screams of soldiers and horses alike were drowned out by the roar of the water as it came crashing down upon the enemy, destroying every one of them.

At first the enormity of what had happened was overwhelming. With thudding hearts the Israelites watched the bodies of dead soldiers wash against the shore. But then the reality of their deliverance and of what God had done through his servant Moses took over. The party began.

The singing! The dancing! Miriam's feet moved in time with the tune ringing in her head as she remembered that celebration. It had been her finest, most joyful experience in leadership. She had taken a tambourine in her hand and lifted it above her head, her feet stomping the earth. With all the women—thousands of them—following her, she sang out her joyful song of praise to God: "Sing to the Lord, for he is highly exalted! The horse and its rider he has hurled into the sea!"

As the echo of that song from long ago faded and the reality of her recent behavior and present circumstances confronted her, Miriam sadly shook her head. God had allowed her not only to help lead the Israelites, but to be one of his spokespersons. She was a prophetess, speaking the word of the Lord to the people. How, after personally experiencing such joy in ministry and after witnessing God's power at work through her humble brother, could she have been so critical and fostered such vain notions?

It had been eating at her for a while, that Cushite wife of his. As Miriam watched from the opening in her tent, she saw Moses lean down to listen to his wife. A smile broke out on his face, and they exchanged warm laughter. Then he turned to watch his wife as she sauntered away with a basket balanced on her head. Miriam shook her head bitterly.

As the day wore on, Miriam not only fostered the critical spirit growing within her, she involved Aaron, and they began to talk against Moses.

"Aaron! Come and share the fire before my tent with me. I would have a word with you."

Looking as old and weary as she felt herself, Aaron lowered himself to sit before the fire. It seemed they had wandered in the wilderness for a lifetime.

"What is it, Miriam? These old bones need their rest."

"Did you meet with Moses today? Did he listen to your counsel?" she demanded.

"He was busy with tribal matters, sister."

"Well, he had enough time to chat in the middle of the day with that Cushite wife of his!" Miriam spat.

Moses's choice of a mate had long disturbed both Aaron and Miriam. Moses may have lived in other cultures, but to marry a foreigner when he had women from twelve Israeli tribes to choose from galled them. That and the constant wandering in the wilderness brought their patience to the limit.

"What would Moses have done without our leadership assistance for all these years? For all his expensive Egyptian education, it sure didn't make much of a speaker out of him! He had to have *you* speak for him in Egypt, Aaron! Wouldn't a more aggressive leader better lead these fickle people who always seem to be complaining?

"Has the Lord spoken only through Moses?" she continued. Her question came out as a challenge, and the two siblings eyed each other in the flickering firelight.

"No, sister," Aaron said, sitting up straighter and meeting her eyes. "He has also spoken through *us*. God assigned us both as leaders *with* Moses when we escaped from Egypt."

Miriam pressed ahead, making her case. "We are both God's messengers as a prophet and prophetess, and we are Moses's *elder* siblings, after all!"

As their egos inflated, they boldly compared their gifts of prophesy to those of Moses and harshly criticized his choice of a wife.

God heard them. And Miriam had been caught in her sin like a snared rabbit. It was far too late to take back her foolish words.

Miriam broke out in a sweat as she recalled God's voice on that day. He had spoken to her and Aaron before in dreams and visions, and God had given them his words to declare to the people. However, that day, God spoke aloud to Miriam and her two brothers: *"Come out to the tent of meeting, all three of you."*

Trembling, they had gone to the tent in the center of the camp, and God came down in a pillar of cloud and spoke to Aaron and Miriam.

"When a prophet of the LORD is among you,
   I reveal myself to him in visions,
   I speak to him in dreams.
But this is not true of my servant Moses;
   he is faithful in all my house.
With him I speak face to face,

clearly and not in riddles;
he sees the form of the LORD.
Why then were you not afraid
to speak against my servant Moses?"

Numbers 12:6–8

God's description of his intimate relationship with Moses and the harsh reality of his anger burning on behalf of his humble servant struck Miriam to the core of her being. Her punishment was swift, and for a little while, she looked death in the face. When God left them, Miriam was covered with leprosy, her flesh partially eaten away.

Terrified, Aaron turned to Moses and begged for forgiveness for the sin he and Miriam had committed. Acknowledging Moses's influence with God to change the course of things, he begged Moses not to allow her to stay in such a horrible condition.

Miriam narrowed her eyes as she checked the position of the sun. In just another hour or so a full week would have passed since the sobering events of that day. Miriam looked down at the clenched hands in her lap and slowly opened her fingers. Her hands were wrinkled and worn, but they were whole. A tear trickled down her cheek, and, swallowing hard, she thought about Moses's response to her plight. He had every right to be furious with her, because she had tried to usurp his leadership. At the very least he could have lectured her about respecting his wife, let alone about his undeniable calling from the Lord God. But he had done none of that. Instead, he had shown his love for her. He cried out to the Lord on her behalf.

"God, please heal her!"

God did not immediately restore her to her normal way of life; he decreed that she should be cast outside the encampment for seven days . . . alone and in shame.

It had been a long, lonely, and sometimes frightening week, but she was to be restored to her people soon. Restored. Forgiven. With a grateful heart, she wept for joy.

Digging Deeper

I chose to tell this story from the perspective of Miriam at the end of her chastisement, as she might have recalled the events of her life. To be honest, I used to struggle with the ending, feeling frustrated that God singled out Miriam instead of Aaron and "zapped" her for punishment. Upon closer study, however, I discovered some important thoughts and information I want to share with you.

Miriam was a woman of influence. She came from a family of faith and was used by God to be a leader. Since she was from the tribe of Levi, she had a godly heritage and from an early age had witnessed God at work within her family. God even gave her the gift of prophecy and appointed her to a position of leadership. Another interesting fact is that she was the first female singer recorded in the Bible. (How wonderful that her first recorded song was in praise to the Lord.) When she led the women in song and dance following the Red Sea escape, Scripture says that all the women followed her. She was the key woman of influence among her people.

The leadership "pecking order" was clear. Throughout the recorded history of the Israelites' bondage and deliverance from Egypt, it is apparent that Moses was God's chosen individual to lead the children of Israel. Many years later, the prophet Micah wrote the words of the Lord listing the three leaders God sent before the people to lead them out of slavery. God said: "I sent Moses, to lead you, also Aaron and Miriam" (Micah 6:4).

Miriam is listed third, but hey, she's in there! However, in Numbers 12, where their sin and God's judgment are recorded, her name is clearly listed first, leading me to believe that she was the instigator in the conflict.

I found some interesting notes lending credence to my theory that Miriam was the instigator when I was studying a tome by Rabbi Joseph Telushkin on biblical literacy. A Hebrew scholar, Rabbi Telushkin states: "The text's internal evidence does offer two suggestions that Miriam was the primary offender. First, the verb used to describe their initial comments is the feminine singular, *ve-teddaber* ("and she spoke"). Second, her name is given first, even though when Miriam and Aaron are mentioned together on all other occasions, his name comes first."[1]

Moses had not been "lording" his authority over Miriam and Aaron. Just the opposite was true. Numbers 12:3 states: "Now Moses was a very humble man, more humble than anyone else on the face of the earth."

Moses could have been vain over so many things: his background as a prince of Egypt, his formal education, which was far superior to that of any other Israelite, his awesome position as leader of the nation of Israel, or the many miraculous things God had done through him. Instead, he was the most humble guy in the world.

No wonder God got so mad. He would not allow the harsh criticism of his most faithful servant (especially by someone who should have known better) to go unpunished.

I don't need to worry if God was "fair" or not. Scripture clearly says that God is faithful and just and that if we confess our sin, he washes away our unrighteousness (1 John 1:9). In Genesis 18:25 Abraham asks, "Will not the Judge of all the earth do right?" That means I can trust God's actions—even if I don't totally understand them. It also means that when I blow it, like Miriam did, forgiveness and restoration are possible for me, too.

I can't imagine that it took very long for Miriam to confess her sin before God. I wonder if her heart-cry was anything like David's after he was caught in the sin of adultery.

> Have mercy on me, O God,
> according to your unfailing love;
> according to your great compassion
> blot out my transgressions.
> Wash away my iniquity
> and cleanse me from my sin. . . .
> Surely you desire truth in the inner parts;

you teach me wisdom in the inmost place.
Cleanse me with hyssop, and I will be clean;
wash me, and I will be whiter than snow.
Let me hear joy and gladness;
let the bones you have crushed rejoice. . . .
Create in me a pure heart, O God,
and renew a steadfast spirit within me.
Do not cast me from your presence
or take your Holy Spirit from me.
Restore to me the joy of your salvation
and grant me a willing spirit, to sustain me.

Psalm 51:1–12

Miriam's week of isolation was probably the wisest thing God could have prescribed for this talented, aggressive, type-A-personality woman. It gave her time alone with him. I figure a contrite Miriam had herself a one-on-one retreat with God, and I'm sure she was never the same again.

What happened to Miriam after her restoration? I studied to find out about Miriam's life after she was brought back into the camp. The only other references are to when she died and where she was buried, and a sobering epitaph in Deuteronomy 24:9 that says, "Remember what the LORD your God did to Miriam."

What? Not concentrate on her obedience as a child by the Nile River? Her tremendous leadership with the women? Her powerful gift of prophecy, or even her lovely solo voice? Remember her downfall? After giving that some prayerful thought, I realized that God used the word "remember" because obviously there's something from this story I ought to apply to my own life.

How can this story apply to your life?

Keep your focus on God. God's presence was before the Israelites in the form of a pillar of cloud during the day and a pillar of fire by night. I wonder if Miriam got so used to his presence that she took its awesomeness for granted and later on took her eyes off it entirely and focused on herself and her own ambitions. She used to take great joy in her Lord and his leadership. But then she changed her focus and decided to be the boss herself.

We live in an exciting time in history, when women in this country can aspire to virtually any position. As God allows many of us to assume positions of leadership, whether in our communities, churches, workplaces, or ministries, we don't have to be consumed with promoting ourselves or elevating our positions of authority. If we make him Lord of our life and keep him ever before us, he can open astonishing doors of opportunity (like giving me the opportunity to write this book) and fulfillment we never dreamed possible. As Christians, or followers of Jesus Christ, God's Son, we are his personal representatives, and we are on assignment to make him (not ourselves) visible to a lost and dying world.

I've lived long enough to see some pretty famous Christian leaders blow it. Dynamic ministries suffered or totally bit the dust because somewhere along the line those leaders took their eyes off Christ and concentrated on themselves. Some became greedy for fame, others for money or illicit sex. And not only were their personal reputations ruined, but the testimony of Christ they had proclaimed was damaged because they wanted to be the boss.

Actually, I have quite a lot in common with Miriam. I too grew up in a family of faith and have a godly heritage. I too have the privilege of "up front" ministry as a speaker and storyteller, and I, like Miriam, have a famous sibling in ministry who both speaks and writes. (That's my awesome and darling older sister, Carol Kent, by the way.) I also have a controlling, hard working, type-A personality that I need to continually surrender to the Lord. I don't know about you, but I'd much rather learn from Miriam's mistake than have God deal with me regarding my own. I'm so thankful that God paused long enough in recording Miriam's story to say "remember." How about you?

Bite your tongue! Ever wish you could take back harsh thoughts or bitter words you've used against someone? I have. Frankly, they were usually said because I felt superior to the person or wanted to control a situation.

I sure am grateful for forgiveness.

I know that a story like Miriam's is a haunting one, but God can use it to reveal our own pride and foolish actions. The good news is he loves us so much—even enough to chasten us if necessary. And if we confess our sin, he is faithful and honorable to forgive us and wash away our unrighteousness (1 John 1:9).

The best way I can describe God's forgiveness is to tell you about forgiveness that was extended to me when I didn't deserve it.

I was homesick. Deeply, painfully, overwhelmingly homesick.

My husband was in the army, and we were sent far from our home state of Michigan to Ft. Polk, Louisiana.

I desperately missed my mother. I remembered her tenderness and the times she had sacrificed for me. I thought of the countless mornings I had come down the stairs and found her on her knees at our old, worn-out couch, praying out loud for her children. I more than missed her. I was haunted by the memory of how many times I had made her cry when I was a teenager.

I was a good student, a class officer, and very involved in my high school. Life was exciting, and I was a platform person. I had a lead role in every play our school produced from my freshman to my senior year. I loved the spotlight. But our house had no stage or spotlight. I lived in a parsonage with a family of eight on a limited budget. I resented the workload that came with being one of the oldest, and I was unhappy with the scarcity of money. I objected to my parents' strict rules and to the curfew they enforced on me. I verbally abused my mom.

"Why are you so unfair? I have the lead in the school musical, and you make me come home from the play party by midnight!

Are you trying to humiliate me in front of my friends, or is it that you don't trust me?"

"Why do I have to vacuum the whole downstairs before I leave for school every morning? Then when I get home from school, there's a sink full of dirty dishes to wash before we even have supper! What do you do all day anyway?!"

I had many grievances, and when the front door was closed—and especially if my dad wasn't there—I had a harsh and selfish tongue that I exercised on my mother. For some reason she let me get away with saying those hateful things, but sometimes she cried.

Years later, there I was, a grown woman, established in my own home, far away, missing her—and miserable that I had made her grieve.

Four years passed. My husband was nearing the completion of his military service, and we needed to find a home and office space for his legal practice. Deciding to come home to Michigan for a quick trip during my Easter break from teaching, I wrote ahead to my mom, inviting her to come down from the Upper Peninsula to meet us. She drove the six-hour trip downstate all by herself so we could be together, and it was a wonderful reunion.

The next day I found my mom sitting in a rocking chair in the home where we were staying. Her head was back and her eyes were closed. She was sound asleep. I stood there in the doorway and watched her for a while.

I love you so much, Mama, I thought. *I've missed you so.* Standing there, I realized the time had come for me to make something right that had been very wrong for a long time.

Walking into the living room, I knelt beside her chair and gently laid my elbow in her lap. As she woke up, I rested my head against my arm. She tenderly stroked my hair as though I were a little girl again.

"Oh, Mom, I've missed you so much!"

"I've missed you too, honey," she responded, caressing my cheek.

I straightened to look up into her eyes. "Mom, there's something that's been bothering me for a long time, and I have to ask you to forgive me."

She looked at me and said, "Forgive you? Jennie, whatever for?"

"Oh, Mom, for all those times I made you cry when I was a teenager. I didn't understand that when you were strict, you were trying to protect me. I was so full of myself. I didn't have any real understanding of Dad's ministry or that it was our family ministry too. You had a house full of children, and it was my part of the ministry to vacuum every morning. When dirty dishes were waiting in the sink after school, it was because you'd been dishing out prayer, counseling, and apple pie to spiritually needy people all afternoon. I was so selfish. I hurt you so many times. Please forgive me, Mama. I am so sorry."

Through fresh tears of her own, my mother embraced me and quietly replied, "Oh, my dear Jennie. I love you and I forgave you so long ago, so very long ago."

Many years have passed since that refreshing day, but I have been grateful countless times since for the lesson Mother taught me by modeling God's forgiveness. When I go to my Heavenly Father with a broken and contrite heart and say, "Oh, God, I'm so sorry. I blew it. I have hurt you again. Please forgive me," the Savior looks at me through all the love that prompted him to go to the cross of Calvary and says, "Oh, my child, I love you. I have loved you since before you were born, and I paid the price for that so long ago. You're forgiven."[2]

A Passionate Prayer

Dear Heavenly Father, thank you for Miriam's story. So often I'm just like her—serving you joyfully one moment and expecting praise and recognition the next. Please forgive me for the times I've ignored your presence and purpose in my life and instead, focused on myself.

Thank you for the awesome privilege of being your representative here on earth. Please guard my heart from the temptation to promote myself instead of you.

Also Lord, will you guard my lips? Keep me from using them spitefully against others. Keep me from criticizing those you've placed in authority over me.

And please give me the courage to say "I'm sorry" to those I have wronged and give me the grace to forgive those who have hurt me, knowing how unconditionally you have loved and forgiven me.

I love you Lord. I pray this prayer in the precious name of your Son, Jesus. Amen.

The Scripture Reading: Numbers 12:1–16

Miriam and Aaron began to talk against Moses because of his Cushite wife, for he had married a Cushite. "Has the LORD spoken only through Moses?" they asked. "Hasn't he also spoken through us?" And the LORD heard this.

(Now Moses was a very humble man, more humble than anyone else on the face of the earth.)

At once the LORD said to Moses, Aaron and Miriam, "Come out to the Tent of Meeting, all three of you." So the three of them came out. Then the LORD came down in a pillar of cloud; he stood at the entrance to the Tent and summoned Aaron and Miriam. When both of them stepped forward, he said, "Listen to my words:

> "When a prophet of the Lord is among you,
> I reveal myself to him in visions,
> I speak to him in dreams.
> But this is not true of my servant Moses;
> he is faithful in all my house.
> With him I speak face to face,
> clearly and not in riddles;
> he sees the form of the Lord.
> Why then were you not afraid
> to speak against my servant Moses?"

The anger of the LORD burned against them, and he left them.

When the cloud lifted from above the Tent, there stood Miriam—leprous, like snow. Aaron turned toward her and saw that she had leprosy; and he said to Moses, "Please, my lord, do not hold against us the sin we have so foolishly committed. Do not let her be like a stillborn infant coming from its mother's womb with its flesh half eaten away."

So Moses cried out to the LORD, "O God, please heal her!"

The LORD replied to Moses, "If her father had spit in her face, would she not have been in disgrace for seven days? Confine her outside the camp for seven days; after that she can be brought back." So Miriam was confined outside the camp for seven days, and the people did not move on till she was brought back.

After that, the people left Hazeroth and encamped in the Desert of Paran.

Final Note: When did this thought-provoking story take place? According to the *Baker Commentary on the Bible,* biblical scholars agree that the exodus took place around 1440 BC.[3] If so, the story of Miriam's rebellion took place sometime between 1439 and 1400 BC. (Remember, the number gets smaller as the calendar gets closer to the birth of Christ.)

4

Pride Takes a Bath
A Story about Humility, Healing, and Servanthood

H ey, I am lookin' *good* tonight!"
Sucking in my stomach, I turned from side to side, studying my reflection in the mirror. I was accompanying my husband to a special annual business dinner that evening, and I wanted to look my very best. I wore a dressy suit and had taken special care in doing my hair and makeup. Admiring the result of my efforts, I had the self-satisfied feeling that my husband would be proud to have me on his arm that night.

Hours later and back at home again following the dinner, I washed my hands at the bathroom sink. Seeing my reflection once again, I grinned at myself, feeling pleased that the evening had gone so well, and recalling several compliments on my outfit.

Our daughter, Amber, who was just eight years old at the time, woke up and walked into the bathroom where I was standing. She was flushed with sleep and was warm and cuddly in her long, fuzzy nightgown. She ducked under my arm and I hugged her as she stood in front of me.

"How are you doing, sweetie pie?" I asked, kissing the top of her head.

We could see each other in the mirror before us. Suddenly, her sleepy eyes lit up and she responded with excitement.

"Mom! I finally know what I'm going to get you for Christmas! You're just going to *love* it!"

Not wanting to dampen her enthusiasm but realizing it was only mid-March, I responded, "My, you *are* an early shopper, aren't you?"

Her response was filled with earnest excitement, and one thought tumbled out after another. "Well, it costs an awful lot of money, Mom. It's $19.95. I'm going to need a long time to save up for it. It's okay though," she continued, "because I know I finally thought of something you really *need*. You're just gonna *love* it!"

She paused. "There's just one problem." Her little brow furrowed. "I don't think it's going to be able to be a surprise."

Turning her around to face me, I cupped her precious little face. I told her that I loved surprises and tried to explain that I didn't need expensive presents. "Sweetheart," I said, "homemade gifts made with lots of love are my very favorites."

She shook her head. "No, Mom. I'm sure *this* one will be your very favorite present this year. I *know* you'll love it, so I think it's okay if I tell you what it is ahead of time. See, I can earn the money by Christmas, but I don't know how to order it. The advertisement said I have to call a toll-free number, and I'm not quite sure I know how to do that. Do you?"

A toll-free number? My mind raced. "Yes, I know how to use a toll-free number. But, honey, what could I possibly need that you would order over the phone?"

She exploded with her news. "A GUT BUSTER!! You really *do* need one, don't you, Mom?" She smiled up at me with naive confidence. "I told you it was something you would love to get!"

You've heard the expression, "Out of the mouths of babes"? My daughter's observation and statement of my "need" was not something I really *wanted* to hear, but I had to admit there was certainly some truth in it.

In the Old Testament book of 2 Kings, there is a story about a proud man who had a great need, and because of his willingness to heed the wise advice of a young girl in his household, his life was radically transformed. His name was Naaman, and he was the commander in chief of the army of the king of Aram (Syria). He lived in the royal city of Damascus, where idol worship was rampant and where he personally accompanied his king into the temple of Rimmon. His amazing prowess on the battlefield had made him not only the king's favorite but had earned him respect and popularity among the people. The Bible refers to Naaman as a valiant soldier, but in spite of his wealth, position, and popularity, even the lowliest slave in Syria would not have chosen to trade skin with him. For you see, Naaman had leprosy. He was caught in the grip of a loathsome disease that could eventually rob him of his vigorous strength, ban him from society, and at some point, take his life.

Naaman's Story

Upon entering the opulent sleeping quarters of her mistress, the young girl smiled with delight at the sight of her lady dressed in a lovely new gown. "You called me, ma'am?" she asked politely.

"Yes, child. Come here and help me clasp my necklace," her mistress ordered kindly. "Your master will be home soon, and I want to look my best."

"Master Naaman will think you are very beautiful, my mistress," the girl said sincerely. "You will make his heart sing!"

The woman looked at the girl for a moment and then smiled sadly. "I wish it were as simple as putting on a new gown," she said.

What is it about this young Israelite that prompts such confidences? the woman wondered. The child had been with them

73

long enough to understand not only the inner workings of the household in which she served, but also to recognize the very real agony with which they lived. Naaman's wife had marveled many times at the girl's positive attitude in the face of her own circumstances. Who could have blamed her if she had been sullen in her subservience? She was a spoil of war. But instead of exhibiting bitterness, the child was cheerful and helpful. She was indeed a blessing in their privileged but plagued household.

The girl knelt on the floor beside the woman, who sat with her hands tightly clasped in her lap. Looking earnestly up into her mistress's face, the girl spoke with boldness.

"I know how my master may be made well, mistress."

The woman was startled out of her reverie by the statement and looked sharply into the girl's face. The child's enthusiasm spilled over into her declaration. "If only my master would see the prophet who is in Samaria! He would cure him of his leprosy."

Involuntary hope sprang in the woman's breast as she looked into the sweet face, shining with absolute faith. Could it be that Elisha, this prophet of the Hebrew God, could cure Naaman? Hadn't they tried sacrificing before the sculpted gods in the temple of Rimmon to no avail? As she studied the sweet contours of the face before her, she inhaled deeply and resolved to speak to Naaman about the matter as soon as possible.

"Naaman, my man! What brings you into my presence this morning? Do you have tales of recent border skirmishes that will whet my appetite for expanding my kingdom?"

The king was delighted to see Naaman, but, although his greeting was buoyant, his concern for his servant's physical condition was heightened. It was obvious that the leprous condition of the man standing before him was getting worse.

Naaman bent his considerable frame to bow before his king.

"I would request a personal word with you, my king," he said.

Sensing the intensity of Naaman's request, the king immediately issued orders to clear the room. Naaman then launched into a story about a raid conducted some time earlier that had resulted in a young Hebrew captive being added to his personal retinue of servants. Repeating the girl's claim that the Hebrew prophet Elisha could heal him of his leprosy, Naaman sought the advice of the king.

"Absolutely! You must go!" responded the king. "However, we both know that since you've beaten the tar out of Israel in your recent encounters, they might be a bit reluctant to see you coming! So, my friend, I'm going to send a letter with you to prepare the way." He patted his chest importantly. "They wouldn't dare turn you away!"

He wrote the letter, which said, "With this letter I am sending my servant Naaman to you so that you may cure him of his leprosy." Sealing it with his great royal seal, he handed the letter to Naaman with his best wishes and bid his faithful warrior good-bye.

And so Naaman and his attendants left for Samaria. Expecting to reward the prophet Elisha for his services, Naaman came loaded with 750 pounds of silver and 6,000 pieces of gold, which weighed another 150 pounds. He also brought with him gifts of 10 sets of rich clothing. With his horses and ornate chariots and entourage of servants, Naaman made an impressive sight as he approached the palace of his foe. And he was received with proper pomp and ceremony as an emissary of the nation of Syria. But when the uneasy Israelite king received the letter with the Syrian king's seal upon it, he almost had a nervous breakdown. In great distress, he ripped his royal robes and cried out to his advisors: "Am I God? Can I kill and bring back to life? Why does this man send someone to me to be cured of his leprosy? See how he is trying to pick a quarrel with me!"

When the news of the king's distress reached Elisha, God's prophet, he sent word to the king, asking why he was so upset. Then he instructed the king to send Naaman to him, so he would know there was a prophet in Israel.

How Naaman anticipated his meeting with Elisha! The old man was famous for performing miracles. True, Naaman had heard they were usually to benefit the poor, but he planned to reward the prophet well enough. As his impressive entourage continued on its way, he imagined how the healing would proceed—with pomp and ceremony, no doubt. First there would be official introductions, perhaps a formal presentation of gifts, and then, upon the prophet's satisfaction with the offering, he would begin the healing ceremony. Official protocol was something with which Naaman was very familiar.

A shout from his scout indicating their destination was in sight brought Naaman out of his musings. He crested a small hill, and with an accelerated pulse the veteran soldier surveyed the modest holding before him. Not what he had expected. In Naaman's world, power produced wealth, and this prophet was said to be powerful indeed. But Naaman saw no evidence of wealth before him.

Naaman signaled his horses and chariots to proceed until they stopped at the door of Elisha's house. There they waited for the great prophet to appear.

When the door finally opened, there was no pomp or ceremony. There were no formal introductions. Instead of Elisha himself acknowledging their presence, a simple servant appeared with a blunt message for Naaman: "Go and wash yourself seven times in the Jordan, and your flesh will be restored, and you will be cleansed."

"What?!" Naaman stared in disbelief at the servant. Then his astonishment turned to irritation.

"I have traveled a considerable distance, at great personal expense," he responded in a formidable tone. The servant simply stepped back inside and closed the door.

Turning away from the entrance, Naaman angrily moved an arm through the air, venting his frustration in the presence of his servants. "I was sure that the prophet would present himself to me and that he would wave his hand over the spot and cure me of my leprosy. If *bathing* could cure me," he spat out in derision, "why couldn't I wash in the beautiful, clear rivers in Damascus? What a waste this trip has been! Mount up, men!" he barked. "Get those chariots turned around! We are out of here!"

So Naaman went off in a rage, his sober entourage following behind him.

After a time, he signaled the company to rest and water the horses. Stepping down from his chariot and surveying the company to see that all was well, he wearily seated himself on the rear edge of the chariot and wiped his brow with his forearm. He could feel the blistered, diseased flesh of his forehead, and, burying his head in his hands, he felt his rage give way to the grief of bitter disappointment. What had happened to him? Had he come so far in life, only to end up a leprous, raging madman in the end?

"Excuse us, sir."

Naaman looked up to find his servants standing before him, their expressions wary but filled with concern. These men knew him well, and it occurred to him that they had repeatedly watched him keep a cool head in battle but today had witnessed his hotheaded fury, born of wounded pride and desperation. One servant respectfully spoke for all of them.

"If the prophet had told you to do some great thing, wouldn't you have done it? Doesn't it make sense that since he gave you a simple task instead, you should just do it?"

For a moment, Naaman sat in stunned silence as the truth of those simple statements sunk in. What a fool he had been. His eyes moved from one anxious face to another, and, after a moment's silence, he nodded. Heaving a sigh, he tipped his face to the heavens and felt hope once again.

Standing, he raised an eyebrow and asked his servants, "Are you ready to ride to the Jordan with me? I am suddenly very inclined to take a bath!"

His servants helped Naaman remove the impressive ceremonial garments he had donned for Elisha's benefit and then watched anxiously as he waded into the cool water of the Jordan. When he was about waist deep, he paused to look down at his extended hands, which were scarred by battle and disease. Then he looked back to his men on shore. Giving them a grin and a wave, he called out, "Here goes!"

Inhaling, he dropped his rear end to the river bed, submerging himself to the top of his head. Springing back up, he threw back his head, reached up to wipe the water out of his eyes, and then stretched out those same fingers for inspection. No change.

He looked up at the anxious witnesses on shore and shook his head. Well, the prophet had said to wash himself seven times. Lifting his index finger, he called out, "That was one!"

He dipped again, and again, and again, and again, and yet again, his servants calling out the numbers while he spat out the occasional mouthful of gritty water. Then he closed his eyes, inhaled, and submerged his body for the seventh time.

Pushing himself up out of the water, Naaman knew even before he opened his eyes that he was whole. What was it the prophet had said? *Go and wash yourself seven times in the Jordan, and your flesh will be restored, and you will be cleansed.* Indescribable joy and gratitude overwhelmed him as he raised his hands to push his dripping hair back from his forehead. But the emotion he felt was far more than the joyful realization that he had been healed physically. It was the awesome awareness that the Lord God had cleansed him spiritually as well.

Giving a jubilant shout, Naaman headed for shore and toward his faithful servants, who stared in joyful wonder at his flesh, which had become as smooth and new as the skin of a young boy.

Naaman did not immediately rush home to Syria to show his wife and his king the astounding results of his mission. Instead, he and his attendants headed back to the home of Elisha. This time Naaman was allowed into Elisha's presence, and the radiant new believer stood before the prophet and proclaimed, "Now I know that there is no God in all the world except in Israel. Please accept a gift from your servant."

Elisha stroked his chin as he heard the once-proud captain testify to God's power and offer his gifts. Naaman, who was so used to paying his way, thinking everything and everyone had a price, needed to learn that his new God could not be bought—that God cared far more about the heart of a man than about his outward trappings.

"No," said the prophet. "As surely as the Lord lives, I won't accept a thing."

"But you must! There is silver here and gold, too! I brought new clothing as well. Surely you can use *some* of it!" Naaman urged.

But still Elisha refused.

"Well, if you won't take my gifts, would you allow me, your servant, a special favor? May I take as much of the earth of this place as two mules can carry, for you see, I will never again make burnt offerings and sacrifices to any other god but the Lord. That way I will have holy ground on which to offer sacrifices to God."

Elisha granted his permission, so the ground was dug up by the servants, and the dirt was packed in large bundles and fastened to the backs of two mules. *This is good*, thought Naaman, picturing the special place he would prepare for worship. But thinking about his life back in Damascus reminded him of something that now made him uncomfortable.

"Sir," he asked Elisha hesitantly, "there's one thing that I pray the Lord will forgive me for. You see, part of my life—my job back in Damascus as captain of the army—is to accompany my king into the temple of Rimmon. He leans his arm upon mine to bow before Rimmon, and it is necessary that I bow, too." Naaman's consternation over this dilemma was obvious as he continued, "May the Lord forgive your servant for this."

Elisha studied the earnest new believer who stood with his head bowed before him. He knew that God had singled this man out long before, had given him military victories over the Israelite nation, and had allowed a humbling disease to make him desperate enough to seek out the true God. Pride may have gotten in the way at first, but in the end, Naaman had humbly submitted to God's direction. Elisha knew he could give a long list of do's and don'ts that Naaman would do his very best to follow, but he chose not to. Instead, he simply said, "Go in peace."

A grateful Naaman said a humble and heartfelt good-bye to the prophet Elisha, then turned his chariots around once again and headed for home. This time, his entourage included two mules carrying holy ground upon which he would offer sacrifices to the one true God.

Digging Deeper

As I read and reread this story in 2 Kings 5, I was impressed with how many different lessons can be taught from this one passage. For instance, there are three important references to servants in the story. First, there is the captive girl who had wise advice for Naaman. Second, there are Naaman's servants, who approached him after his fit of temper and gave him counsel. And third, Naaman, the wealthy captain, refers to himself as a servant, after he has become a believer. What a transformation from the proud, controlling man he had once been!

For a better grasp of the story, let's break it down into sections and do a little digging for greater understanding.

The Captain. Naaman was a brilliant leader with a grievous handicap. His great popularity stemmed from his leading the Syrian army to victory over the Israelites, but take special note that verse 1 tells us it was the Lord who had given him the victory over God's own people, who at that time had strayed far from God.

Naaman's desperation regarding his leprosy can be seen by his willingness to take the advice of a young servant girl. But what was his affliction like? In the Bible, the word "leprosy" is used to describe a variety of skin ailments. I believe Naaman's leprosy was a condition called white leprosy because of a description of Elisha's servant Gehazi's condition later on in the chapter. In *Fausset's Bible Dictionary* a graphic description of the condition tells us just how loathsome a disease it was: "Leprosy, beginning with little pain goes on its sluggish but sure course, until it mutilates the body, deforms the features and turns the voice into a croak. . . . Anesthetic elephantiasis (white leprosy) begins in the forehead with shining white patches which burst; bone by bone drops off; the skin is mummy like; the lips hang down exposing the teeth and gums. . . . The leper was a walking tomb."[1]

And Captain Naaman had it. Fausset states that individuals diagnosed with white leprosy could live up to twenty years as their condition worsened. Although Naaman's disease was both disgusting and frightening, it obviously had not progressed to the point that he was banned from Syrian society. (In Israel, however, he would already have been segregated.)

The Captive. It was common for bands of soldiers to go out from Aram (also known as Syria) on raids and bring back slaves. The Bible records that on one such border raid in Israel, the Syrians brought back a young girl who entered into the service of Naaman's family.

I suspect she must have suffered fear and terrible homesickness, but her depression is not recorded for us. What *is* recorded is her assistance to her mistress, her urgent advice, and her enthusiastic testimony of the power of God manifested by the prophet in her homeland of Samaria! I found it interesting that in every translation I read, her sentence in verse 3 is punctuated with an exclamation point! She must have been convincing, because Naaman actually went to his king with her advice, and even the king thought it was worth the trip into enemy territory.

It's remarkable that she even suggested such a healing, because she had never seen or even heard of Elisha healing anyone of leprosy in her homeland, let alone a foreigner. In Luke 4:27 it is recorded, "There were many in Israel with leprosy in the time of Elisha the prophet, yet not one of them was cleansed—only Naaman the Syrian."

It seems to me that the little girl, in spite of circumstances in her life she would not have chosen, was an incredible testimony of God's awesome power. I wonder if I, given her circumstances, would have reacted in such a helpful way.

The Correspondence. Naaman's king not only encouraged Naaman to go and seek out the prophet, but he also tried to prepare the way by sending a letter to the king of Israel. Naaman went with dignity, bearing his sovereign's letter, a company of attendants, and a tremendous treasure of gold, silver, and clothing.

When the king of Israel received the letter, he went berserk, tearing his clothes in consternation, thinking this was a plot to provoke another battle. I figure the king could have been upset for several reasons:

1. Naaman was the very captain who had led the Syrian army to defeat the Israelites!
2. The man had leprosy! In Israel, he already would have been banished to the leper colony, or at the very least would have been required to wear a badge of mourning covering his upper lip.
3. The king of Israel was so content with his idols and so out of touch with the prophet Elisha that as he read the Syrian king's letter, it never occurred to him that the Syrians were looking for an introduction to the prophet. The king figured they expected *him* to heal Naaman, and he tore his clothes and cried out, "Am I God? Can I kill and bring back to life? What are they trying to do—require the impossible of me, just so they have an excuse to attack us again when I can't deliver?"

Elisha heard what was happening and sent word to the king to send Naaman to him, so "he will know that there is a prophet in Israel" (v. 8). (It was perhaps as much a reminder to the king of Israel as it was a lesson for Naaman.)

How often have we reacted to situations like the king did? Frantically trying to figure out a way to deal with a crisis, only to realize we are helpless in our own strength?

The Command. When Naaman reached Elisha's house, he had great expectations that included not only a cure, but also ceremony and some semblance of protocol. At the very least, he expected to be received by the prophet personally. Instead, the door opened, a messenger stepped outside (probably Elisha's servant, Gehazi), and without any word of greeting or welcome, blunt instructions were issued. The curt instructions were simple enough—too simple, in fact. Naaman exploded with rage and spouted off to his attendants what his dramatic expectations had been. Verse 11 says, "I thought that he would surely come out to me and stand and call on the name of the LORD his God, wave his hand over the spot and cure me of my leprosy!" I think it sounds like he wanted a little magic or ceremonial hocus-pocus, doesn't it? Can't you hear him—"I've already traveled for days, and he expects me to go even further to the Jordan River? If I had wanted a bath, I could have taken one at home."

He then hit the road. Scripture says "he turned and went off in a rage" (v. 12). For all his effort, nothing had gone as he had expected, and he was furious.

The Counselors. Under normal circumstances, if your boss was furious about something, wouldn't you try to keep your distance until he or she cooled off? Well, Naaman's employees didn't. God had gifted Naaman with wise and faithful servants. First, the little maid, and then servants who had witnessed both his excited urgency regarding his mission and his temper tantrum when all did not go as he had expected. It had been a long trip already (approximately 110 miles from Damascus to Samaria), and who could have blamed the servants for wanting to head home? But they cared enough for their boss to approach him respectfully and offer a quiet, thought-provoking question and some sensible advice. Their servant leadership stopped Naaman in his tracks and caused him to turn his heart and his entourage back on a path that would lead to both his physical and spiritual healing.

The Cure. Naaman swallowed his pride, returned to Samaria, and continued on for an additional twenty-five miles to the Jordan River. Once there, he obeyed the instructions from the prophet. God honored his obedience and Naaman's skin became new—like the tender, unblemished skin of a little child. Can you imagine? "It's gone! Look! I am free of this thing! I am whole!"

It occurred to me that Naaman was accustomed to hand-to-hand combat and no doubt carried scars from his years as a warrior. Isn't it interesting to realize that those scars must have been erased right along with his disease?

His cure required humility rather than a showy act of bravado. It required faith rather than a bargain between two powers. It required obedience rather than a payment for services rendered. The end result of Naaman's humble willingness to comply with God's directive was far more than he had ever hoped for, because in addition to new skin, he received new life; he accepted the one true God.

The Confession of Faith. Even more dramatic than the miracle of Naaman's physical healing was the miracle of his spiritual rebirth. A powerful Gentile and an idol worshiper was spiritually transformed. My brother-in-law, Kelly Carlson, is a pastor and biblical historian who graciously allows me to pick his brain now and then. He had this comment when we were emailing about this passage: "Naaman's story is an incredible example of irony, in that the traditional enemy of God's people is made to travel his former military path to humbly ask for a new lease on life. No ritual or membership in the Jewish club [is required], just direct connection with the living God."

Naaman's public testimony of his belief in and commitment to the one true God was far stronger than that of any Israelite at that time, except for the prophet Elisha himself. Naaman's radical spiritual transformation was evidently a humbling experience, because when he went back to the prophet to say a heartfelt thank you, this once-proud man referred to himself five times as a "servant" (vv. 16–18). What a switch!

How can this story apply to your life?

Bottom line, Naaman accepted God at his word and took the action needed to apply his belief to his life. Result: he was radically changed, inside and out. One of the great lessons here is that when we apply God's Word to our lives, he can radically affect us, too!

Also, this story teaches that salvation is for *everyone*, not just for a particular race or type of person. I was impressed that when this new believer explained that part of his job description back home was to accompany the king to the temple of Rimmon, Elisha didn't complicate his new walk of faith with a bunch of rules.

"What, Naaman!? Don't you know that as a new believer you can no longer smoke, dance, drink, or escort the king to the temple? And by the way, no tattoos or earrings either!"

Nope. Elisha simply saw Naaman's sincere desire to worship God and didn't give him a list of do's and don'ts. Instead, he said, "Go in peace" (v. 19). So often in my zealous evangelistic efforts I have been quick to dictate actions and lifestyles that will make someone "look" like a good Christian, without allowing the Holy Spirit to bring conviction in the controversial areas of his or her life. Do you do this, too?

So often God uses trying circumstances in our lives to draw us to him. Naaman was a powerful man who chose to lean on God in a time of despair and weakness. When you find yourself in a hopeless situation, choose to lean on God. Accept him as Naaman did. God will lead you through your difficulties.

Our son, Josh, was born with a congenital birth defect. He was missing one rib in his back and half of the connecting vertebrae. The condition never stopped him for a minute—he was active and surprisingly agile. He was a great student and an avid soccer player. Then when he was sixteen, the bottom fell out of his life. He grew five inches in one year, and his spine twisted. When the orthopedist told us that Josh needed radical spinal surgery, Josh's first comment was, "Can it wait till summer?"

"No, Josh," came the reply. "Your spine is twisting so quickly that if we wait, you will be a handicapped adult."

His spine was on a fifty-five-degree angle.

The second opinion concurred with our specialist, and the next ten days were a frenzied blur of preparation. There was the MRI experience, donating blood in advance of the surgery, touring the critical care unit of DeVos Children's Hospital in

Grand Rapids, where Josh would be cared for, and making arrangements with his teachers for a long absence.

We were terrified. We hated our situation. We feared the risk of paralysis the doctor warned us about. We worried about the school Josh would miss and that he might never play soccer again. We were saddened that he would never qualify for military service. We had just come through some other stresses in our lives. We needed a rest. Why in the world would God allow something like this to happen now? With nowhere else to turn, we cast our anxiety on the Lord and hung on to him for dear life.

We never dreamed that this difficult experience in our lives would be such a blessing.

Like Naaman before his leprosy was diagnosed, sixteen-year-old boys don't need God for much. They've got their sports, their strong body, their brain, and just maybe a girlfriend. If they accepted Jesus as a little kid, like Josh did, they've got their ticket to heaven. What more could they need?

Our son had a crash course *we* never would have chosen. It was in "Run to Jesus, 101" and it profoundly affected his life, his manner, his testimony. He's a different kid, and we wouldn't trade him back for the old one, even if it meant being able to avoid the trauma of that year. Neither would Josh.

He sent an email update to his cousin, JP, several months after his surgery:

> *I've got two titanium rods supporting my spine now, and my curvature is corrected to 38 degrees. I'm not going to pretend this whole deal hasn't been painful. I've been doing a lot of thinking and praying lately, and I think that I look at life a lot differently than I used to. I realize that some of my friends are wasting their lives on things that aren't worth their time and that they hurt people around them without even caring. It's not that I see the world in different colors or anything, but I'm sure a nicer person than I used to be!*

I'm thankful for the lessons God has taught me
through all this, and want to communicate to my
friends how good he's been to me.
Thanks for praying for me. Please keep it up.
Your cousin, Josh D.

Interested in a postscript? Josh graduated tenth in his class, played varsity soccer his senior year, earning academic all-state honors and the distinction of being named the "Most Improved Player." He went on to the University of Michigan where he is active in Campus Crusade and leads several Bible studies on campus. As he did with Naaman, God worked through a physical condition to draw a young man unto himself. God did far more than we asked in Josh's life, and through it all he taught us to trust him.

A Passionate Prayer

Dear Heavenly Father, so often I'm just like Naaman. I want you to work dramatically in my life to solve my problems, without personally being willing to humble myself or be obedient to your direction in my life.

Please forgive me . . . show me . . . teach me . . . and help me be willing to set aside my own pride and those things that fill me with self-importance to follow you. Lord, help me to serve you with a willing and humble heart in the days ahead, no matter what my circumstances may be. Help me serve others in such a way that my words and actions draw them unto you.

In the precious name of Jesus, Amen.

The Scripture Reading: 2 Kings 5:1–19

Now Naaman was commander of the army of the king of Aram. He was a great man in the sight of his master and highly regarded, because through him the LORD had given victory to Aram. He was a valiant soldier, but he had leprosy.

Now bands from Aram had gone out and had taken captive a young girl from Israel, and she served Naaman's wife. She said to her mistress, "If only my master would see the prophet who is in Samaria! He would cure him of his leprosy."

Naaman went to his master and told him what the girl from Israel had said. "By all means, go," the king of Aram replied. "I will send a letter to the king of Israel." So Naaman left, taking with him ten talents of silver, six thousand shekels of gold and ten sets of clothing. The letter that he took to the king of Israel read: "With this letter I am sending my servant Naaman to you so that you may cure him of his leprosy."

As soon as the king of Israel read the letter, he tore his robes and said, "Am I God? Can I kill and bring back to life? Why does this fellow send someone to me to be cured of his leprosy? See how he is trying to pick a quarrel with me!"

When Elisha the man of God heard that the king of Israel had torn his robes, he sent him this message: "Why have you torn your robes? Have the man come to me and he will know that there is a prophet in Israel." So Naaman went with his horses and chariots and stopped at the door of Elisha's house. Elisha sent a messenger to say to him, "Go, wash yourself seven times in the Jordan, and your flesh will be restored and you will be cleansed."

But Naaman went away angry and said, "I thought that he would surely come out to me and stand and call on the name of the LORD his God, wave his hand over the spot and cure me of my leprosy. Are not Abana and Pharpar, the rivers at Damascus, better than any of the waters of Israel? Couldn't I wash in them and be cleansed?" So he turned and went off in a rage.

Naaman's servants went to him and said, "My father, if the prophet had told you to do some great thing, would you not have done it? How much more, then, when he tells you, 'Wash and be cleansed'!" So he went down and dipped himself in the Jordan seven times, as the man of God had told him, and his flesh was restored and became clean like that of a young boy.

Then Naaman and all his attendants went back to the man of God. He stood before him and said, "Now I know that there is no God in all the world except in Israel. Please accept now a gift from your servant."

The prophet answered, "As surely as the LORD lives, whom I serve, I will not accept a thing." And even though Naaman urged him, he refused.

"If you will not," said Naaman, "please let me, your servant, be given as much earth as a pair of mules can carry, for your servant will never again make burnt offerings and sacrifices to any other god but the LORD. But may the LORD forgive your servant this one thing: When my master enters the temple of Rimmon to bow down and is leaning on my arm and I bow there also—when I bow down in the temple of Rimmon, may the LORD forgive your servant for this."

"Go in peace," Elisha said.

Final Note: The story of Naaman, captain of the army of Aram (Syria), which is recorded in 2 Kings 5, was probably written before 586 BC.[2] Second Kings records the stories of two national tragedies: the fall of Israel, the northern kingdom, and the fall of Judah. It also gives a powerful record of the extensive ministry of Elisha. The story above took place toward the end of Elisha's life.

5

Dear Abby
A Story about Holy Living While in a Difficult Relationship

Heidi is one of the most delightful women I've ever known. We met about fifteen years ago at a women's retreat where I was speaking. She had a joyful countenance and an infectious laugh, and she was a natural leader. It was obvious that her committee loved and respected her. We spoke over the phone several times prior to that weekend, but when we met in person, a precious friendship was born.

As the years went by, Heidi and I grew to be as close as sisters, often sharing both our joys and our sorrows with one another. Given her joyful personality, I was shocked and sobered to learn that years before, while growing up in a Christian home, she had been sexually molested by an older brother. Then, as a young woman, she fell in love and married Kevin, a handsome young man who loved her dearly but who had a tendency to be very controlling and painfully frugal. They had two children, a lovely home, and good jobs. But things were far from perfect.

While in her late thirties, Heidi started having flashbacks from her abusive childhood that terrified her. Kevin tried to be supportive at first, but he soon came to resent the process she needed to go through for healing and tried to control her even more. Their relationship deteriorated and was almost lost, but in desperation, Heidi took action. She asked several close friends (including me) to pray. She found a Christian counselor who helped her begin the careful steps needed to confront the past, offer forgiveness where it seemed undeserved, and actively trust God to restore her marriage. She and Kevin, on the advice of their counselor, separated for six months while both went to counseling and started "dating" each other all over again. Kevin learned that it was actually fun to spend money to take Heidi out for dinner, and Heidi learned to quit focusing on the past and to embrace the future God had for her as an individual and as part of a couple. Kevin and Heidi learned to forgive each other, and God restored not only their marriage and ministries, but their passion as well.

I'm so grateful to know Heidi and Kevin, and I have taken great joy in watching how God uses them to encourage others who may be struggling with something in their past or in their marriage. In 1 Samuel 25 there is a story about a wise and beautiful woman who was in a very difficult marriage. Her name was Abigail, and she, too, refused to live her life as a victim. Her story, like Heidi's, should give hope to each of us.

Abigail's Story

Making her way to the house from the noisy stalls where sheep were being herded for shearing, Abigail paused to sweep her gaze across the vast expanse of her husband's empire. It had been a very profitable year for Nabal, and his livestock had increased to the mind-boggling number of three thousand sheep and a thousand goats. Sensing that the completion of the enormous task of shearing was in sight, servants and additional hired hands were exhausted but in good spirits. It would soon be time for celebration.

Abigail's eyes then moved to focus on the mountainous area just beyond their holding at Carmel and scan the craggy horizon for evidence of their protectors. She had caught glimpses of David's band in the weeks past and had been informed by her husband's herdsmen that their profitable flocks were in part the result of the protection David and his men had offered against thieves and bandits.

Also from the tribe of Judah, David was their kinsman, and, although the old prophet Samuel had anointed him as their future king, David was presently in exile in the mountains near Carmel. Stories had circulated about David escaping the murderous King Saul on several occasions, and he and his army were camped around and about them here.

As she turned back toward the house, Abigail's reverie was rudely interrupted by an all-too-familiar voice cursing in the distance.

"Get out of my sight, you lazy good-for-nothing!" Nabal shouted as an unfortunate servant scurried away. A string of profanities followed, and then he bellowed, "Where is my wife? Where's my wine?"

Abigail winced at his tone, and then composing her beautiful features, she inhaled deeply and prepared to greet her husband.

Wide awake later that night after meeting Nabal's demands for food, wine, and sexual pleasure, Abigail slipped from his bed. She averted her eyes from his obese nakedness, which gave clear evidence of his indulgent lifestyle, and blew out the small oil lamp that still flickered on the bedside table. Quietly stepping to the window, she stared out at the outline of the mountains in the moonlight. Sadness overwhelmed her for a moment at the circumstances of her life, but only for a moment.

Her marriage had been arranged, and her father, who truly cared for her, had thought the wealthy Nabal quite a catch for his daughter. When news of the betrothal had circulated throughout the village, some had envied the beautiful, capable young woman. Others, who had worked for Nabal or had done business with him, pitied his bride-to-be, but her happiness was not at issue. The bargain was made.

Nabal's household was large, and the young bride soon found her place. Because of Nabal's vain irresponsibility and weakness for wine, some decisions regarding his estate fell to Abigail, and his own servants came to her for direction. In spite of the shame and embarrassment caused by her husband's despicable behavior and verbal abuse, Abigail thrived under her responsibilities. A capable manager, she was both smart and clever, and in dealing with a difficult husband and a large household, she had to use every resource available to her. She also exercised forgiveness. To stay with a man who was cruel and foolish, she practiced forgiveness daily, trusting God for the strength, wisdom, and ingenuity to face each new day. She was a woman of faith. She knew God had a plan for her life.

"Lady Abigail! I must speak to you!"

The urgent tone of Nabal's servant was not lost on Abigail. Turning from instructing other servants who were preparing food for the celebration, she hurried to the man.

"David sent messengers from the desert to give our master his greetings, but he hurled insults at them. These men were very good to us—they did not mistreat us, and when we were out in the fields near them nothing was missing. They were a wall around us all the time we were herding our sheep. When they requested food, since it is our feast time, Nabal refused them! He not only refused them any kindness, he insulted them and their master, David. They have left angry, and I fear for all our lives! Nabal is a wicked man, and we can't talk any sense into him! Please think of what you can do, or surely we are all lost!"

Abigail groaned aloud at her husband's selfish stupidity, visualizing the possible ramifications. Her mind raced. There was no time to waste lamenting Nabal's foolishness. She flew into action, praying she could save both her household and her husband's hide as well.

Looking Nabal's servant squarely in the eyes, she issued several orders.

"Listen to me carefully and make haste. Take five sheep that have been slaughtered for the shearers and load the meat on donkeys. I will need other pack animals to carry a large quantity of foodstuffs and servants to lead them. I will also require a donkey for myself. See that they are made ready. Now, go quickly!"

Grateful for the abundance of food that had been prepared ahead for the feast time, Abigail turned to her servants. "We must hurry!" she called out. "Pack two hundred loaves of bread and two skins of wine. Count out one hundred raisin cakes and two hundred cakes of pressed figs. Measure out a bushel of roasted grain and pack everything on the donkeys. I want you to start out with these gifts ahead of me, and do not be afraid. I will make myself presentable and follow you. I will speak to David myself, and may God go before us all. Now hurry!"

David was furious.

"Nabal said *what*? Why that selfish ingrate! He knows we have aided him for many weeks! It's been useless—all my watching over his property so that nothing was missing. Put on your swords! I want four hundred men to go with me to Nabal's holding and two hundred to stay here with the supplies. I swear that by morning not one male belonging to Nabal's household will remain alive!"

David set out with his men from their mountain camp, angry but also discouraged. Political exile on the run with an army of six hundred men to feed was no small responsibility, but added to that, he was dodging repeated assassination attempts by King Saul. He also was deeply grieving the death of the prophet Samuel, who had anointed him king. Dealing with these challenges without his wise counselor, he found it was easier to doubt his calling from God. "At least by taking revenge on Nabal, my men will eat," he muttered to himself.

"Look, sir! Someone approaches!"

After issuing orders to set the food-laden caravan in motion, Abigail hurried to make herself ready to meet David. "Oh, God, put the right words on my lips and cause David to listen!" she prayed. Then, mounting her donkey, she prodded the animal ahead until she overtook those who had left before with their heavy burdens. "Keep coming!" she urged them. "I will go before you to speak to David."

As she guided her donkey into a mountain ravine, her breath caught in her throat at the formidable sight of David and his army making their descent toward her. With her heart thundering in her chest, she quickly dismounted and approached him, bowing down with her face to the ground at his feet. Without preamble and without looking up, humble words poured from her lips.

"My lord, let the blame be mine alone. Please let your servant speak to you, and listen to what she has to say. May my lord pay no attention to that wicked man Nabal. He's just like his name, which means fool, and folly goes with him. But as for me, your servant, I did not see the men you sent."

Remaining on the ground, she dared to raise her head and look at David. He was ruggedly handsome, his complexion ruddy from the sun and his hair was blowing in the wind. Most importantly, he had not drawn his sword and was staring at her intently. Swallowing hard, she continued the speech God had laid on her heart for David.

Intent on his mission, David was in no mood to see a woman approaching from the direction of Nabal's holding. She was obviously a young woman of affluence, judging from her garments and boldness. However, to his surprise, she fell at his feet in abject humility, pleading for his attention and, of all things, indicating that she was the old coot's *wife*! When she raised her face to look at him, he was struck by far more than her great beauty. Intelligent eyes met his, and the words she spoke pierced his heart.

The woman gestured to an impressive string of pack animals being led into the ravine. "Please let this gift be given to your men for their nourishment, and forgive your servant's grave offense," she implored. Then, turning back to David, she stunned him with her intense words of prophecy and wisdom.

"The Lord will make a lasting dynasty for you, David, because you fight the Lord's battles. Let no fault be found in you as long as you live. Even though someone is seeking to take your life, you will be protected by the Lord your God. However, the lives of your enemies God will hurl away as stones from the pocket of a sling. When the Lord has done for you every good thing he promised concerning you and has appointed you leader over Israel, you, my master David, will not have on your conscience the staggering burden of needless bloodshed from having avenged yourself."

Abigail finished her impassioned speech and dropped her eyes for a moment before quietly adding, "And when the day comes that the Lord grants you success, please remember me, your servant." She could feel her cheeks burning, but it didn't matter. If David accepted her apology, Nabal's life and the men of their household might be spared. She clasped her trembling hands together as she waited for his response.

David stared in wonder at the woman's bent head. He had been blinded by rage, but she had reminded him of his noble calling by God and had caused him to reckon with the grievous sin he had almost committed. With sudden clarity he realized that this woman had been sent by God to stop him in his tracks, and with that understanding, he was overwhelmed with gratitude. Reaching up to comb back his hair with his fingers, he closed his eyes in wonder at the disaster that had been averted.

"Praise the Lord God for sending you to meet me!"

Abigail's chin bobbed up, and her eyes widened in startled amazement.

"May God bless you for exercising your good judgment, which has kept me from bloodshed this day. I was bent on vengeance against Nabal and the men of his household, which would have displeased the Lord God. You have stopped me in time, and I am sincerely thankful."

With waves of relief washing over her, Abigail released the breath she had been holding, and a tremulous smile lit up her beautiful face. After a pause, she blurted, "Are your men hungry, my lord? There is fresh bread and fruit and mutton for roasting."

David's intensity dissolved and a grin split his rugged countenance in response to her question. "Hungry? Ma'am, they're *starving!*"

Then, sober once more, his gaze met hers. "I accept this gift from your hand with a grateful heart. Go back to your home in peace."

Abigail, her eyes shining, nodded and turned to issue orders to her servants to unpack the donkeys. She turned once more to nod to David, mounted her own donkey, and went on her way.

David's eyes followed Abigail as she left. What a remarkable woman. Thank God she had come! God had called him to far greater things than settling scores with the likes of foolish men like Nabal.

All the way down the mountain, Abigail rehearsed in her mind the report she would give to Nabal. Would he understand how close he came to losing his life and the lives of so many others?

Music and laughter spilled from the house as she arrived. Inside she found a drunken Nabal hosting a feast truly fit for a king. Abigail stood there, quietly observing his excesses for a few moments, then turned away, grateful he had not noticed her arrival. This was no time to talk to him. Morning would come soon enough, and with it, sobriety.

It was late morning when Abigail approached Nabal. Bleary-eyed from overindulging the night before, he was a sorry sight.

"Husband, I would like a word with you."

Raising his eyebrows seemed an effort, but he managed. "So there you are, my pretty little disappearing wife." He snatched her wrist and dragged her close enough for her to smell his foul breath. "How gracious of you to seek my company this morning when you neglected your wifely duties at my banquet last night."

Without cowering or showing her revulsion, Abigail spoke with the dignity and respect he did not deserve. "I was on a mission of extreme importance, Nabal, a mission that saved your life."

"Eh?" He shoved her away and reached for a small loaf of dark bread on the table beside him. Taking a bite, he eyed her suspiciously as he chewed.

"Nabal, I was told that you turned away David's men with insults."

"Riffraff!" Nabal snorted. "That band of beggars expected compensation for guarding my flocks. Did I hire them? No way! I sent the buzzards packing!"

"Nabal," Abigail persisted quietly, "are you aware that because you offended him, your lavish party last night was almost interrupted by David and four hundred of his men bent on slaughtering not only you, but every male in your household?"

Nabal froze in the process of taking a bite, holding the bread in midair. "Four hundred men? Surely you are mistaken."

Somber eyes looked back at him. "No, Nabal. Your servant warned me that he feared for your life and for others. So I packed food and met David and his army in the ravine. I pleaded for forgiveness. God put the right words on my lips and caused David to listen in spite of his anger against you. He was on his way to kill you, Nabal. God spared you from David's hand."

The enormity of her words sank into Nabal's heart like a rock, and he tasted fear on his tongue instead of bread. Breaking out in a cold sweat, he stood to reach out to Abigail for support and then suddenly clutched at his chest. "My heart! My heart! Wife, it fails me!"

Abigail screamed for help as she eased his collapse to the ground. She frantically shoved aside his cloak to place her ear against his chest. The faint beating reassured her somewhat, as did the shallow breath coming from his mouth, but he did not say another word. He was like a stone.

Ten days later, Nabal died.

"Sir! Your scout is approaching from Carmel!"

David looked up, squinting as he focused on the pass leading into the camp, and then waved in welcome. "What have you learned, my friend? Any new news from Saul's camp?"

"Nothing in that regard, sir, but I do have news that should interest you. Nabal is dead."

David's head jerked up. "How can that be?" When his servant relayed the details he had learned, David sat in stunned silence for a few moments and then asked, "When was his collapse? Was it truly just a day after I was to take his life?"

David stood and walked a few feet, then turned back to his scout. "Vengeance was the Lord's, not mine," he said, shaking his head in wonder. "How I praise the Lord God that he kept this sin from my hands!"

Later that evening, as sleep eluded him, David found himself thinking of Abigail. She had been something else, all right—beautiful, courageous, and an amazing diplomat. He smiled, recalling the high color in her cheeks and the intensity of her speech. And the food! The memory of the provisions she had given them made his mouth water.

Nabal probably never even appreciated the gem he had in her, he found himself thinking. How refreshing it would be to carry on an intelligent conversation with such a woman. He sighed heavily, suddenly feeling very lonely.

Staring into the darkness, he pondered Abigail further. In spite of being married to a renowned idiot, she was faithful to and protective of him. She had put herself in the line of fire for the worthless lout. She understood the importance of godliness, and she had lived it in a difficult marriage.

Then a thought hit him like a bolt of lightning: Abigail was single.

His heart hammered with excitement as he thought about the possibility of making Abigail his own. Then doubts came. *I'm an outlaw. Why in the world would a wealthy, beautiful young widow consider becoming my wife? What kind of life could I offer her?*

But then he recalled her understanding of God's plan for his future, and it gave him hope. One of the last things Abigail had said to him was, "When the day comes that the Lord grants you success, please remember me, your servant."

He smiled in the darkness.

"My lady! There is a messenger here to see you!"

Abigail turned her attention from estate matters to follow her servant to the door. Since Nabal's death, many things had required her attention. This was probably one more neighbor offering condolences.

On the doorstep stood a young man holding a rolled parchment, which he held out to her. "This message is from my master, David," he said, flushing slightly. "He regrets he is unable to speak to you in person regarding this matter, but as you know, it would not be safe for him to come into Carmel at this time. Please consider his request." Bowing a bit awkwardly, he left.

Bemused, Abigail opened the message. Her hands trembled, and her breath caught in her throat. David wanted her to become his wife.

Abigail's first husband had been chosen for her. This time, the choice was hers to make. As Abigail contemplated her life and future, she knew that to turn down David's proposal would leave her a wealthy, childless widow with a comfortable income and a business to run. To accept would be to step by faith into a great unknown to live with an outlaw, albeit one with a heart for God and who was destined to be king.

The memory of David's fierce handsomeness was forever etched in her mind, but what attracted her far more was that he *liked* her mind. And best of all was his genuine heart for God. Deciding to make a brave choice, Abigail prepared for the adventure of a lifetime.

When David's servants arrived in Carmel to bring her to him, she was ready. She summoned her five maids who would be traveling with her and, wasting no time, climbed on a donkey that would carry her to the mountain camp. There she would become the bride of King David.

Digging Deeper

Abigail's story, found in 1 Samuel 25, has every element needed to be entertaining. There's a villain, a handsome hero, a refreshingly intelligent heroine (who happens to be very beautiful), the threat of murder, a mountain hideout, and romance. The bad guy even dies in the end. It has some important lessons for women today as well. Take a look with me at the key elements of the story.

Abigail's marriage was miserable. Nabal and Abigail were ill-matched in an arranged marriage. They were unequally yoked with regard to intelligence, graciousness, wisdom, and godliness.

Nabal's name meant "foolish," and by both word and deed he exemplified his name. A wealthy man, he was likely older than his wife. He had a foul mouth and a drinking problem. He was referred to as "wicked" by his servant. He put great store by his wealth, but he had been given a greater blessing in Abigail that he never appreciated. He treated with brutish contempt strangers who had been kind to him. I hate to think about how he treated his wife behind closed doors.

Abigail's name meant "my father rejoices." In contrast to her husband, she was respected by the servants in her household, and she brought some joy and a sense of order to the place. She also was a forgiving woman. To live with Nabal, she would have had to exercise forgiveness every day. Scripture says Abigail was a woman of understanding, and she used that wisdom to live with a very difficult personality, at a time in history when women were often considered chattel.

Abigail, who was both beautiful and capable, did not wallow in bitterness or self-pity and, in spite of the evil character of her husband, took action that would save his life. Susan Hunt, in her book *Spiritual Mothering*, says, "Abigail's spirit was not bound by her predicament. She was not emotionally paralyzed. She had a freedom to relate to others and to act with precision and quickness in a crisis."[1]

They were Beauty and the Beast. There is no mention of children between them.

Nabal's ingratitude was the last straw. Having been a shepherd as a boy, David understood shepherding. To protect Nabal's vast herds with his army for many weeks was indeed a great service. Nabal should have embraced and rewarded David's men at shearing time, rather than scornfully sending them away.

A godly woman, Abigail had a spiritual understanding regarding David being the anointed of God to be king. Nabal lacked that understanding and spoke about David with contempt, referring to him as a slave in revolt against his master.

When David heard of the offense, it triggered his plan for revenge against Nabal and all the men of his household. When Abigail heard the news, it catapulted her into a life-and-death drama.

Abigail acted independently. It was one thing to take Nabal's drunkenness and bad temper personally, but when his crude manner and selfishness threatened not only his own life, but the safety of the entire household, Abigail drew the line and interceded.

She could have panicked and barricaded herself in the house or organized the servants to fight. She could have argued with Nabal about what he should have done. She could have allowed David's revenge to rid her of Nabal and free her from the shackles of her marriage. Instead she used the wisdom God gave her, and the course of history was changed. She became a peacemaker.

Acting quickly and without Nabal's permission, she took five of the very sheep he had withheld from David earlier, packed a picnic lunch that was meant to feed an army, and had a caravan on its way up the mountain in record time. Full of faith and the fear of the Lord, she faced a handsome, outlaw warrior who was bent on murder. (His good looks are described in 1 Samuel 16:12.) In one of the lengthiest speeches by a woman recorded in Scripture, she encouraged him to refocus on God's sovereign plan for his life and stopped him from committing an atrocity he would later regret. She also made a lasting impression on the future king.

Exit husband #1. The following morning when Abigail told Nabal how closely he came to losing his life and what she had done to prevent the attack, he became violently ill. The passage records that "his heart failed him and he became like a stone" (v. 37). It is likely that he had a stroke. Ten days later he died. The Scripture leaves no doubt regarding the cause of Nabal's death when it says, "the LORD struck Nabal and he died" (v. 38).

When David heard the news, it reaffirmed to him that revenge belongs to the Lord, and he was again grateful that God had led Abigail to stop him from shedding Nabal's blood. He also realized that he desired Abigail for his own wife, if she would have him.

David proposes. It was by proxy. Not very romantic, but genuine. Verse 39 tells us that "David sent word to Abigail, asking her to become his wife." It was common for a representative of the bridegroom to negotiate on his behalf with the family of the bride with regard to the dowry that the groom would pay for his bride. This situation was a little different, however, in that both Abigail and David had been previously married. (He was married to King Saul's daughter Michal, who had been taken from him by her father and given to another man.) Plus, David was financially needy, while Abigail was wealthy.

As the writer of so many beautiful psalms, David had such a way with words that I hope he at least sent a personal letter to Abigail with his proposal. We'll never know.

I am assuming that at least a short time passed between verse 39 and verse 40, where David's servants arrived to pick her up for the wedding, because not only was she ready to go when they showed up, so were five other women!

Enter husband #2. It was in the mountains; Abigail risked her security to partner with David in exile. What do you think she brought to David in marriage? My research repeatedly pointed out that she would have provided him with a rich estate and a new social position, but Scripture doesn't even mention her personal wealth. Instead it stresses her wisdom. Abigail brought to the marriage remarkable faith, beauty, wise counsel, and a history of acting quickly. (Quite an asset for a man on the run!) She believed in God's call on David's life and encouraged him to make right choices.

Abigail's life during those early days with her rebel husband was indeed filled with adventure—including being kidnapped by an enemy army and later being rescued by her husband. (Way to go, David!) While still in exile in Hebron, she bore him a son and named him Chileab, also called Daniel, whom she raised to be a godly man. She lived in polygamist times and had to share David's affection with other wives, but Abigail will forever go down in history as the woman of wisdom and beauty who was married to Israel's greatest king.

How can this story apply to your life?

(1) Choose your mate carefully and prayerfully. Abigail didn't have a choice the first time, but you do! (2) While going through difficult circumstances, it is possible to function with dignity and wisdom, rather than be emotionally paralyzed and held captive by those circumstances. (3) Wise words and actions can promote peace and protect those we care about. (4) Forgiveness enables us to function without anger. (5) God honors those who honor him. (6) Lastly, a hint with humor: the next time you want to make an important appeal to your dad, boyfriend, spouse, or even your grandpa, you might consider following Abigail's example. Include both intelligent conversation *and* the taste of great food. His heart isn't all that far from his stomach! (I guess some things never change.)

It is impossible to read Abigail's story and make light of her life with an abusive husband. Some who read this book will identify with Abigail because they are in a similar situation.

Some of you are suffering from pain in your past, and it is affecting your life and relationships in the present. Perhaps you have suffered physical or sexual abuse, rejection, miscarriage, verbal abuse, divorce, or the loss of a child. You are so wounded and consumed by the past that you're not emotionally or spiritually whole anymore.

Will you consider Abigail's story and allow God to use it to rekindle hope in your life? Take action! First, go to God and ask his forgiveness for taking your eyes off him and allowing the problem to consume you. Then, pray for wisdom. (He promises to give it to us in James 1:5.) Next, assess the situation and make a change! This could mean extending forgiveness and becoming a peacemaker. It may mean a change in attitude. Maybe you need to draw a healthy boundary between you and someone or some place. Perhaps you need to take an action like seeking the advice of a Christian counselor or doing something that will protect your children. But do something! Just be sure that your heart is right with God as you do it. Take heart, dear friend. Look up!

At one point in my marriage, I was dealing with deep anger and disappointment. (I'm not going to elaborate because I don't want you to start measuring whether your pain is greater than mine was, but I will stress that my husband was *not* unfaithful to me or physically abusive.) The thing that upset me the most was that he didn't think what he had done was a big deal at all, and to me it was *huge!* As I struggled to "get a grip" emotionally, I opened a little devotional book and was struck with the message. In essence, the meditation admitted that it is impossible for us to forgive on our own. But because we are God's children, we have access to his forgiveness, which makes all the difference. The meditation went on to say that when we extend sincere forgiveness to the offender, God will not give us a case of "holy amnesia," but he will drain the pain from the wound.[2] I remember dropping my face into that book and tearfully asking God to give me his ability to forgive and to please drain away the pain.

God answered that prayer. It didn't happen instantly, but I did experience his peace in place of the emotional storm. As the days passed, my relationship with my husband mended, and my husband was so touched by my new attitude that he in turn shocked me with an act of sacrifice that I will never forget. God honored my action and my faith, and he healed our relationship completely.

A Passionate Prayer

Dear Heavenly Father, thank you for encouraging me with Abigail's story. Please forgive me for the times I've wallowed in my circumstances rather than keeping my eyes on you and following your direction. Please breathe your wisdom into me and let it be apparent in my speech and in my actions. Help me to honor you with my life and to be open to your leading.

Father, I struggle with old hurts. Please give me your capacity to forgive, because I simply can't in my own strength. And Father, please drain the pain from those old wounds and heal me from the inside out! Help me to focus on the future that you have for me instead of on the past. Thank you for loving me and for the plan you desire to work out in my life.

In the precious name of Jesus, Amen.

The Scripture Reading: 1 Samuel 25:1–42

Now Samuel died, and all Israel assembled and mourned for him; and they buried him at his home in Ramah. Then David moved down into the Desert of Maon. A certain man in Maon, who had property there at Carmel, was very wealthy. He had a thousand goats and three thousand sheep, which he was shearing in Carmel. His name was Nabal and his wife's name was Abigail. She was an intelligent and beautiful woman, but her husband, a Calebite, was surly and mean in his dealings.

While David was in the desert, he heard that Nabal was shearing sheep. So he sent ten young men and said to them, "Go up to Nabal at Carmel and greet him in my name. Say to him: 'Long life to you!

Good health to you and your household! And good health to all
that is yours!

"'Now I hear that it is sheep-shearing time. When your shepherds
were with us, we did not mistreat them, and the whole time they were at
Carmel nothing of theirs was missing. Ask your own servants and they
will tell you. Therefore be favorable toward my young men, since we
come at a festive time. Please give your servants and your son David
whatever you can find for them.'"

When David's men arrived, they gave Nabal this message in
David's name. Then they waited.

Nabal answered David's servants, "Who is this David? Who is this
son of Jesse? Many servants are breaking away from their masters
these days. Why should I take my bread and water, and the meat I
have slaughtered for my shearers, and give it to men coming from
who knows where?"

David's men turned around and went back. When they arrived,
they reported every word. David said to his men, "Put on your
swords!" So they put on their swords, and David put on his. About
four hundred men went up with David, while two hundred stayed
with the supplies.

One of the servants told Nabal's wife Abigail: "David sent
messengers from the desert to give our master his greetings, but he
hurled insults at them. Yet these men were very good to us. They did
not mistreat us, and the whole time we were out in the fields near
them nothing was missing. Night and day they were a wall around us
all the time we were herding our sheep near them. Now think it
over and see what you can do, because disaster is hanging over our
master and his whole household. He is such a wicked man that no
one can talk to him."

Abigail lost no time. She took two hundred loaves of bread, two
skins of wine, five dressed sheep, five seahs of roasted grain, a
hundred cakes of raisins and two hundred cakes of pressed figs, and
loaded them on donkeys. Then she told her servants, "Go on ahead;
I'll follow you." But she did not tell her husband Nabal.

As she came riding her donkey into a mountain ravine, there
were David and his men descending toward her, and she met them.
David had just said, "It's been useless—all my watching over this
fellow's property in the desert so that nothing of his was missing. He
has paid me back evil for good. May God deal with David, be it ever

so severely, if by morning I leave alive one male of all who belong to him!"

When Abigail saw David, she quickly got off her donkey and bowed down before David with her face to the ground. She fell at his feet and said: "My lord, let the blame be on me alone. Please let your servant speak to you; hear what your servant has to say. May my lord pay no attention to that wicked man Nabal. He is just like his name—his name is Fool, and folly goes with him. But as for me, your servant, I did not see the men my master sent.

"Now since the LORD has kept you, my master, from bloodshed and from avenging yourself with your own hands, as surely as the LORD lives and as you live, may your enemies and all who intend to harm my master be like Nabal. And let this gift, which your servant has brought to my master, be given to the men who follow you. Please forgive your servant's offense, for the LORD will certainly make a lasting dynasty for my master, because he fights the LORD's battles. Let no wrongdoing be found in you as long as you live. Even though someone is pursuing you to take your life, the life of my master will be bound securely in the bundle of the living by the LORD your God. But the lives of your enemies he will hurl away as from the pocket of a sling. When the LORD has done for my master every good thing he promised concerning him and has appointed him leader over Israel, my master will not have on his conscience the staggering burden of needless bloodshed or of having avenged himself. And when the LORD has brought my master success, remember your servant."

David said to Abigail, "Praise be to the LORD, the God of Israel, who has sent you today to meet me. May you be blessed for your good judgment and for keeping me from bloodshed this day and from avenging myself with my own hands. Otherwise, as surely as the LORD, the God of Israel, lives, who has kept me from harming you, if you had not come quickly to meet me, not one male belonging to Nabal would have been left alive by daybreak."

Then David accepted from her hand what she had brought him and said, "Go home in peace. I have heard your words and granted your request."

When Abigail went to Nabal, he was in the house holding a banquet like that of a king. He was in high spirits and very drunk. So she told him nothing until daybreak. Then in the morning, when

Nabal was sober, his wife told him all these things, and his heart failed him and he became like a stone. About ten days later, the LORD struck Nabal and he died.

When David heard that Nabal was dead, he said, "Praise be to the LORD, who has upheld my cause against Nabal for treating me with contempt. He has kept his servant from doing wrong and has brought Nabal's wrongdoing down on his own head."

Then David sent word to Abigail, asking her to become his wife. His servants went to Carmel and said to Abigail, "David has sent us to you to take you to become his wife."

She bowed down with her face to the ground and said, "Here is your maidservant, ready to serve you and wash the feet of my master's servants." Abigail quickly got on a donkey and, attended by her five maids, went with David's messengers and became his wife.

Final Note: Abigail's story was written sometime during the tenth century, BC. It takes place shortly after the death of Samuel the prophet, which brought to a close the period of the judges. The nation of Israel had become a monarchy, with Saul as the first king and David as the second.

6

Seeking God's Face
in the Rat Race of Life
A Story about a Seeker

As I was skimming through my email one day, a forwarded story caught my eye. Since my own daughter was a sophomore in college at the time, this email was particularly arresting. It seems that a young college student had several problems that she knew would be difficult for her parents to accept, so after struggling with how she could communicate these matters to them, she decided to write a letter that went something like this:

> Dear Mom and Dad,
> I want to update you a little with what's happening in my life. I'm in love! I met Rudy at a little pub near campus where a lot of students hang out. He's a waiter there. Rudy quit high school after eleventh grade and got married, but he and his wife divorced a year after their baby was born, and he's been getting his life back together.

We've been a couple for almost two months and hope
to get married this summer. You should probably know
that I've dropped out of school and plan to move into
Rudy's apartment. (I think I'm pregnant.) I know none
of this is what you would have planned for my life, but I
hope that somehow you'll understand.

She continued the letter on the next page.

I sure love you, Mom and Dad—and not one word
that I wrote on the front page of this letter is true!
However, it is true that I got a "C" in German and I
flunked Statistics. I've been wildly busy and am working
hard, but my other bad news is that I'm out of money
and will need more for my second-semester tuition.[1]

Pretty sneaky! She made bad news sound like good news,
which made it much easier for her parents to swallow. I promptly
resolved *not* to forward the story to my own offspring, but got
to wondering why the girl had chosen to misrepresent herself.
Was she afraid that the truth would result in rejection by her
parents or perhaps an angry rebuke? Whatever her reasoning,
she certainly wanted to change their perspective!

I think most of us have struggled at one time or another with
being caught up in the rat race of life to the point of misrepresenting
ourselves to others. We long to be successful in our relationships,
our work, our politics, and in our communities. We hide our hurts,
our habits, and our handicaps by putting on a good face, and even
those closest to us may be unaware of our inner struggles.

John Powell wrote a little book entitled *Why Am I Afraid to
Tell You Who I Am?* The answer to that question is found a bit
later in the book: "Because you might not like who I am, and
that's all I have."[2]

Isn't that the truth?

There's a fascinating story in Scripture about a man caught
up in the rat race of life. In fact, many people thought he was

a little rat himself! He was a Jewish man who worked for the Roman Empire, and he often misrepresented himself—for personal profit. His story is found in Luke 19:1–10. His name was Zacchaeus.

Zacchaeus's Story

Zacchaeus counted the last of the coins the heavily robed Jew across the table had given him. The man was furious but had paid up nonetheless, and Zacchaeus had to stifle a gleeful chuckle. He certainly took pleasure in taxing the Pharisees; they were so self-righteous. He was tempted for a moment to hand back one silver denarius just to see the fellow recoil at the thought of touching the coin after Zacchaeus had! *Nope*, he thought, snorting slightly. *Wouldn't want to contaminate the poor fellow. I'll just keep his money!*

The disgruntled man turned and left, and Zacchaeus tucked the coins in his bag. Rising, he smoothed the wrinkles out of his fine garment and admired the heavy gold medallion hanging from a chain around his neck. *Life is good now that I'm rich*, he told himself, stepping to the doorway. Or was it? None of the townspeople ever invited him to eat with them. No one ever stopped by just to visit.

His attention was captured by several people racing by his establishment. Following them with his eyes, he saw that a large group of people had gathered farther down the street. People seemed to be coming from every direction to join the crowd. Stepping out into the street, he collided with a young boy who was running by at full speed.

"Uumph!" Zacchaeus recovered quickly enough to grab his assailant before he could dart away.

"You wait just a minute, boy," he said. "What's going on down the street?"

The lad, who stood almost eye to eye with the small man, halted just long enough to say, "It's Jesus! He's coming through

Jericho!" Then, wresting his sleeve away from Zacchaeus, he was on his way again.

Jesus. Zacchaeus stood for a moment, taking in the news. A curious longing welled up inside him, almost making his chest hurt. He had heard things about Jesus. Jesus had healed the sick and fed the hungry. He had confronted the Pharisees and religious leaders. He had befriended sinners and had eaten with tax collectors. Zacchaeus paused just a moment longer before he impulsively turned toward the growing mass of humanity. He had to see Jesus for himself.

Jericho was a bustling and prosperous city. With a spring-fed water supply, it was a lush, green community rising out of the bland, dusty desert that surrounded it. In this center of trade and commerce, Zacchaeus was a powerful man. He liked it when rich men in the marketplace would nod and step aside for him to pass. He didn't fool himself by thinking they were being friendly; he knew they despised and feared him. But as long as they treated him with respect and were lining his pockets with gold, he told himself it was enough.

People hadn't always feared Zacchaeus. His childhood had been a struggle. To his great chagrin, as he grew older he stayed small. Dwarfed by his peers, he was the brunt of jokes and was the last to be chosen in games. The pain of those childhood memories went deep, and the years that went by never erased them.

But although Zacchaeus may have been small, he was smart. As he and his peers grew older, he figured out a way that would not gain him popularity or friendship but would put the snobs and bigots at his mercy, and make him a very wealthy man in the process.

Jericho was under Roman control and was subject to heavy taxation. The Jews in Jericho objected to those taxes because they supported a government that worshiped idols. But in spite of their objections, the Jews were still forced to pay. Of particular irritation to them was that the Romans hired *Jewish* men to collect those taxes. Considered traitors by their fellow Jews, the tax collectors not only collected enough to fulfill Rome's requirements but also additional tax to provide a generous income for themselves.

It was the perfect job for Zacchaeus. What he lacked in stature, he made up for in cunning and manipulation. He was so good at his work that he soon climbed to the top of his field. He now was a chief tax collector, and he had grown men shaking in their sandals. He had made a rich living for himself and was wealthy and powerful. But he was also an unfulfilled, lonely man.

"Make way! Excuse me! Step aside, sir! Do you mind? You're standing on my cloak!"

Exasperated, Zacchaeus shoved his way to the edge of the sea of people now crowding the street. In the frenzy, nobody stepped aside for Zacchaeus but instead pushed and shoved. Disheveled and frustrated, he muttered to himself, "You'd think people would show some respect!"

Zacchaeus's lonely, sinful heart beat fast as he struggled to get through the crowd. It was no use. He couldn't see over the people and he couldn't get through. At this rate, he would never even be able to catch a glimpse of Jesus.

But Zacchaeus didn't give up. He stopped to think about the route Jesus would take passing through the city, and then he started working away from the crowd. It was difficult—like swimming against a strong current—but he figured that if he could just get ahead of the people, he could secure his own spot on the sidelines.

Reaching the open street, he surveyed the area, looking for the right spot to position himself, and then had a brilliant idea! Growing close to the road was a sycamore tree. Why, if he climbed the tree, he would have the best view in the city!

Zacchaeus hoisted up his fine garments, reached for a limb, and felt for a foothold. With a grunt he heaved himself to the level of the first branch and reached for the next. His sandals weren't much protection, and the bark scraped his toes, but in his excitement to see Jesus, he was hardly aware of the discomfort.

He did realize that perching in a tree was a bit undignified for a chief tax collector, but who would notice him up there anyway? Everybody would be watching Jesus.

The crowd was getting closer. Zacchaeus lifted a hand to shield his eyes from the mid-morning sun as he searched the approaching crowd for Jesus. Then he saw him as the crowd made way for his passage through the street. As people reached out to touch Jesus, Zacchaeus was strangely moved by his kindness amidst all the confusion. Then Jesus stopped.

He looked up and made eye contact with Zacchaeus, and Zacchaeus found it impossible to look away. He had never seen Jesus before, but it was as if Jesus recognized him and could see everything from his painful childhood to his wicked, greedy, sinful adult heart. The crowd watched Jesus as he walked to the sycamore tree.

He called Zacchaeus by name. By *name*. Zacchaeus was stunned.

"Zacchaeus," Jesus said, "come down immediately. I must stay at your house today."

With his pulse racing, Zacchaeus scrambled and scraped his way down the tree and led Jesus to his home.

Now when the people saw this, they started muttering and complaining amongst themselves, saying, "He has gone home with a sinner! Why in the world would Jesus seek out someone like Zacchaeus? Why would he want to spend time with that little weasel?" Gathering outside of Zacchaeus's house, they waited for Jesus to emerge.

Inside, a man was opening his heart to the Son of God. The fact that Jesus desired a friendship with him, in spite of his sin and his rotten reputation, broke down his defenses. In the presence of the holiness of Jesus Christ, Zacchaeus was confronted with his own life and was deeply remorseful for his misdeeds. The salvation and forgiveness he received that day so profoundly affected him that he in turn offered startling proof of his conversion to the people outside.

"There they are!"

As the door opened and Jesus and Zacchaeus stepped outside, they seemed to be in deep conversation. Zacchaeus looked at Jesus, the Savior of his sinful soul, the author of his changed life, and then turned to look into the faces of the people who had gathered. How could they ever understand what the Son of God had accomplished in his heart that day? Reaching between the folds of his tunic, he felt for his money bag, which hung from his leather girdle. Turning back to Jesus, he held it out.

"Look, Lord! Here and now I give half of my possessions to the poor, and if I have cheated anybody out of anything, I will pay back four times the amount."

"What did he say?" The murmuring of the people raised several decibels. "Can you believe that? Will wonders never cease!"

Jesus smiled at the sincerity of his precious new follower. "Today salvation has come to this house, for I have come to seek and to save what was lost."

Zacchaeus had been determined to seek the face of Jesus that day. How little did he realize that the Son of God was seeking *him*.

Digging Deeper

I've wondered what earnest words were spoken in Zacchaeus's home that day. It was kind that Jesus dealt with him privately, rather than in front of the crowd. Zacchaeus must have seen his life for what it really was and must have been overwhelmed with the forgiveness and new life that Jesus offered. But no matter what actual words were said, that visit with Jesus radically changed his life.

Just how bad was Zacchaeus? Probably pretty bad. I did a little research on taxation during this time in history. In *The New Manners and Customs of Bible Times* I learned that "Roman officials would sell the right to collect taxes in an area to the highest bidder. The tax commissioner (chief publican) would then have to supply a certain amount of money. He would employ local people as the collectors, and both commissioner and collectors would tax excessively so that they made a good living as well as passing on what was required by the government. Zacchaeus as chief publican admitted fraud by restoring goods fourfold."[3] Zacchaeus was a head honcho. He was a big-time power broker. Another source told me that "Jews in Jesus' time were probably paying between 30 and 40 percent of their income in taxes and religious dues. Not surprisingly, tax collectors were despised by their fellow citizens who viewed them as mercenaries working for the Romans."[4]

So how bad was Zacchaeus? Bad. But the point is, Jesus loved him. No matter how good or bad, tall or short, smart or simple, beautiful or plain we are, Jesus loves us, died to pay the price for our sin, and desires to give us new life in him.

What did the people see in the tree? A small man in fine garments, perched on a limb. They recognized him as the hated tax commissioner.

What did Jesus see? Zacchaeus. Someone very lost and in need of a Savior. While the crowd saw Zacchaeus's small stature, wealthy trappings, and awkward pose, Jesus recognized his spiritual neediness and initiated a life-changing friendship with him.

When God looks at you and me, he doesn't just see our outward appearance, complete with the smile we may have pasted on our face for the benefit of our neighbors. He sees our heart. Have you opened your heart and life to him yet?

How can this story apply to your life?

Zacchaeus took three actions that would radically change his life that day. Those very same actions can radically change your life.

He went out of his way to see Jesus. When his plan was thwarted by the crowd, Zacchaeus didn't give up and go on with his day. He got creative.

How many times have you been interrupted from spending time with God by the phone or doorbell ringing, the needs of your child, or just the rush of life?

Get creative!

Preprogram your car radio so you can easily punch in Christian radio programming while you're in your car. Keep a small case of CDs or cassettes in the car for easy access. Use time on the road to listen to Scripture, inspirational speakers, or praise music.

Sign up for a weekly Bible study at a time that's convenient for you—and with a group who will lift you up and encourage you. There are in-depth studies, couples studies, Bible coffees, and Bible studies for women who want to lose weight together.

And when time alone with God is a challenge, be willing to go out of your way to be with him. This may be as simple as turning off the television and retreating to your bedroom to spend time in prayer or in his Word. It might mean spending your lunch break in the city park with your Bible and your heart open to what he has to say to you. As I tap out this chapter on my laptop, I am camping alone at a Michigan state park, away from my family, email, and the telephone, for the express purpose of spending time alone with God. I have sensed his presence here with me in precious, unmistakable ways, but it took planning and time sacrificed from other things and people to be here.

A friend of mine told me that she communicates best with God while in the bathtub. She said, "I can't pretend to be anything I'm not, and there's nothing I can hide!" (I think Zacchaeus's heart must have felt just that exposed before Jesus that day.)

When spending time alone with God poses a challenge, get creative.

He responded immediately when Jesus called his name. Zacchaeus forgot the crowd, scrambled down the tree, and gladly welcomed Jesus into his home. Jesus only had to call him once.

Do you remember calling your child repeatedly to come downstairs, only to get the response "Just a minute!" or no response at all—that is, until you raised your voice and yelled until you had his or her attention?

One Wednesday evening I found my son, Josh, to be particularly irritating and unresponsive. In addition to acting immature, he had neglected to take out the garbage until I had reminded him three times.

I made the comment (with a sigh) that I hoped I survived his adolescence. Highly offended, he responded by adamantly saying that after his fifteenth birthday on the following Saturday, he would no longer be an adolescent.

"Ha!" I responded.

"It's true," he insisted. "I'm going to get all this out of my system by Saturday. I'm just going to have a big blowout of adolescence and it will be over—I'll be mature and attentive. You'll see."

Then, after a moment's thought, he added with a grin, "Course, Mom, you might be in for a couple of rough days on Thursday and Friday!"

Can you imagine how God must feel some days when he's trying to get our attention? I'm afraid I've given him some pretty rough days.

He allowed his relationship with Jesus to affect his relationship with others. "Look, Lord, here and now I give half of my possessions to the poor, and if I've cheated anyone out of anything, I will pay back four times the amount."

I did a little research and found that Zacchaeus did *more* than what was necessary. Jewish law stated that ordinary robbery must be restored at double value (Exodus 22:4). If the thief voluntarily confessed, he had to pay back the original amount taken plus one fifth! (Leviticus 6:5; Numbers 5:7).

Zacchaeus's commitment to Christ probably meant his financial ruin. But where he used to get his self-esteem from power and money, he found his completeness in Christ.

Does your relationship with Jesus cause others to recognize you as a Christian, as part of God's family? Are you seeking God's face, his friendship, his presence, in the busy race of life you're living?

Eternal success and fulfillment have nothing to do with how tall or short, rich or poor, homely or gorgeous, bad or good, or simple or smart we are. It has everything to do with accepting Christ as Savior, experiencing his forgiveness, and serving him with a pure heart.

Do you know him as your Savior?

Well, he's calling your name, and he wants to go home with you and be a part of your life. Just like he paused to target Zacchaeus up in the tree, he wants a relationship with you. He knows who you are, and he wants to complete the work he's started in you. Yes, he's calling your name.

When I started getting my nails done at a local salon, a young technician named Sandy was recommended to me. When I met her, my first reaction was that she was pretty rough around the edges. My second reaction was that she was one of the most tenderhearted young women I had ever met. Sandy didn't realize that she was a "seeker," but she was.

Getting a manicure is quite an intimate procedure. You sit at a narrow table across from the technician, with your hands extended, and this close atmosphere breeds confidences. As I started coming for regular appointments, I asked Sandy about herself, and the tale she told was sobering and complicated. She was living in an out-of-wedlock situation with a young man who had recently been released from jail. He no longer had a driver's license, and he depended on Sandy for transportation to and from his job as a dishwasher and anywhere else he wanted to go. It was commonplace for him to get high or drunk in the evenings and weekends, and although Sandy genuinely cared for him, she saw herself in a dead-end relationship. Her need for Christ was so apparent.

As the weeks and months went by, I prayed for Sandy and came to genuinely love her as a friend. I often scheduled my appointments before speaking engagements, and she would regularly ask, "Well, Miss Jennie, just where are you flying off to this weekend?" I'd name the place and she would say, "And just what are you going to talk to those women about this week?"

There, in a busy salon at a manicure table, I had the opportunity to share bits and pieces of the story of how I came to know Jesus Christ and the change he has made in my life. Sandy's eyes would get watery, and she'd say things like, "I wish I knew God like that, but he wouldn't know what to do with me! I'm such a sinner."

"Oh, Sandy, we all are sinners."

"You don't understand, Jennie. I've been promiscuous. Once I even was afraid I might have AIDS. I've made some pretty rotten choices in my life. I'm not exactly material that God would be looking for."

"You're so wrong, Sandy. You're exactly the reason he sent Jesus to earth, and he loves you just as you are. I'm praying for you, my friend."

She hugged me and said, "Good. I really need those prayers."

Sandy eventually broke up with her boyfriend. After a short time she met someone new, and after several months, they moved in together. Ray was good-looking and hard-working. He was divorced and the father of two little girls. Sandy confided to me that she loved it when the girls would visit. "I don't think I can ever have a baby of my own, Jennie. I haven't used birth control for years. I'm going to pour all the love that I can into those little girls."

Several months later I walked into the salon to find her extremely stressed. When we sat at the table, she gripped my hands, leaned toward me, and started to cry. "Jennie. I'm pregnant!" she whispered. "Nobody knows, not even Ray or my mom. I can't have this baby, Jennie. I'm so afraid Ray will be mad and leave me. I have to get an abortion. I have no other choice."

I gripped her hands. "Please don't do that, Sandy. You once told me that you never thought you'd be able to have a baby. I know this isn't how you would have planned it, but God has allowed you a very precious gift. You may not ever have that chance again, Sandy."

God had cleared out our usually busy corner in that salon, and for the first time, we had a measure of privacy. Before I left, I put my arms around Sandy and prayed that God would help her do the right thing.

She visited the abortion clinic but decided against the abortion. She would have her baby whether Ray stayed or not. He stayed.

As her pregnancy progressed, her family gave her a baby shower, and I tucked a small devotional Bible in with my gift.

Then, when she approached her final months, Sandy asked if I would be willing to drive to her home for my manicures. "I don't want to lose touch with you, Jennie," she said. I didn't want to lose touch either.

Summer arrived and with it a ten-day conference in Canada where I would be speaking. I was in high gear as I prepared to be gone from home for that long, and one of the things on my last-minute list was a manicure at Sandy's. She was due to have the baby while I was gone.

When I arrived, she was in tears. "Ray doesn't love me, Jennie. He's only stuck around because of this pregnancy, and I know he'll take off when the baby's born. There's no way we're ever going to be a real family." She covered her face and cried.

I had never met anyone who needed Christ more, and yet, I'm ashamed to say, I was so caught up in the rat race of my own life and ministry that I missed the opportunity God offered me. I remember quoting a few soothing Scripture verses to Sandy and putting my arm around her and praying for her before I left, but *I never actually asked her if she wanted to open her heart to Jesus,* the only One who could truly heal her broken heart.

I drove into my driveway, only to be confronted by my conscience. I had suitcases to pack and a plane to catch, but I bowed my head in the car and prayed, "I just blew an opportunity to introduce someone to you, Father. Please give me another chance. If you do, I promise that I won't waste it."

Eleven days later when I got back home, I called Sandy to see if she had a boy or a girl. "Neither!" she laughed over the phone. "This kid is happy as a clam right where he is!"

I asked if I could come over.

"Sure," she said. "You can come right now."

When I arrived, Sandy was cheerful and upbeat. Her manicure table was set up and as she worked, we chatted about my trip. Finally, I couldn't delay my real purpose for being there any longer.

"Sandy, I regret something I didn't do the last time I was here."

"I can't even imagine what that could be," she responded.

I sighed. "You were so emotionally and spiritually needy when I was here, Sandy."

Her hands stilled. Looking up, her eyes filled with tears. "I know, Jennie. I still am."

"You need Jesus, Sandy. He's the only One that can fill up the emptiness in your heart."

She nodded.

"Go and get the Bible I gave you, okay?" She got up and brought back the book. I had to chuckle when she said, "I started reading it, but I'm sure hoping you're not going to quiz me on it or anything."

"No, Sandy, but I am going to tell you the story of Jesus and show you some things from the Gospel of John. It's a love letter from God to you. Look here. It says in chapter three verse sixteen that God loved the world so much that he was willing to send his only Son to pay the price for our sin and give us everlasting life. The only requirement is that we believe of our own free will in him. The next verse says that he didn't come to condemn the world, but that rather, through him and his provision for us, we can be saved. Do you want a personal relationship with God, Sandy?"

She nodded, her face full of hope. "I need to know him, Jennie. If he'll have me, I want to know him."

Together we prayed, and Sandy opened her heart up to God. By faith, she accepted that Jesus had died to pay for her sins and that he rose again to live in her heart and life. She humbly confessed her sin, and her prayer was so precious that I wept before God with her.

I hugged her good-bye and went home with a light heart. And that evening, God gave Sandy a precious gift. She called me a little later with excitement in her voice.

"Jennie! I have to tell you two things. After we prayed and you left, I was so full of peace and quiet joy inside. Then Ray came home, and he brought me a single rose and told me he loved me. He's never done that before, Jennie. Here I am, huge with this baby, and he says he loves me!"

"I think God must have whispered in his ear that you needed to know that right now, Sandy."

The next day, their beautiful baby daughter was born. Sandy called from the hospital to see if I could come up. Graydon and I headed for the hospital together. The baby was exquisite. Sandy looked exhausted but radiant. Ray looked exhausted and a little wary. Before we left, Graydon asked if he could pray for their little family. Sandy nodded with her eyes shining, and we gathered around the bed.

"Dear Father, thank you for this family and the birth of this precious baby. I ask that she would come to know you as her Lord and Savior at an early age. Please draw this family together, and draw them unto yourself. In the precious name of Jesus, Amen."

There isn't time enough to tell you all that has happened in Sandy's life, but I do want to give you a postscript. She and Ray were married in our backyard, in a beautiful garden wedding that September. I held the baby, and Graydon performed the sacred ceremony. Sandy and I later planned a Christian-book study group that met at my house, and she invited her friends. Two of the women who came were totally unchurched, and they drank up every word.

Since that time, Sandy has given birth to another baby, this time a boy. Life has not been perfect, but she is still growing and still hungry to learn what the Bible has to say to her personally. When I visit her twice a month, I often tell her Bible stories or bring a copy of the current chapter I'm working on for this book. The time is precious to both of us. I love her very much, but Jesus loves her far more than I do.

A Passionate Prayer

Dear Heavenly Father, I don't want to be satisfied with just a glimpse of you now and then. I desperately need a relationship with you. I confess that I am a sinner and ask for your forgiveness. Please come into my life and make me new. I welcome you into my home and into my circumstances, as well as into my heart. Thank you for loving me just as I am. Thank you for your gift of salvation! Help me to grow to know you better.
In the name of Jesus, Amen.

The Scripture Reading: Luke 19:1–10

Jesus entered Jericho and was passing through. A man was there by the name of Zacchaeus; he was a chief tax collector and was wealthy. He wanted to see who Jesus was, but being a short man he could not, because of the crowd. So he ran ahead and climbed a sycamore-fig tree to see him, since Jesus was coming that way.

When Jesus reached the spot, he looked up and said to him, "Zacchaeus, come down immediately. I must stay at your house today." So he came down at once and welcomed him gladly.

All the people saw this and began to mutter, "He has gone to be the guest of a 'sinner.'"

But Zacchaeus stood up and said to the Lord, "Look, Lord! Here and now I give half of my possessions to the poor, and if I have cheated anybody out of anything, I will pay back four times the amount."

Jesus said to him, "Today salvation has come to this house, because this man, too, is a son of Abraham. For the Son of Man came to seek and to save what was lost."

Final Note: Jesus met with Zacchaeus toward the end of his journey from Galilee to Jerusalem, where he would be crucified. The story was recorded approximately **AD 60** by Luke, a physician and follower of Jesus Christ.

7

Faith and Friendship Find a Way

A Story about Determined Friendship

When my daughter, Amber, was in nursery school, we lived in an old historic house that was situated on a double lot in the small town of Fremont, Michigan. Every spring my husband took delight in rototilling around the perimeter of the extra lot and planting both flowers and vegetables. There must have been a sale on tomato plants that particular Memorial Day weekend, because he came home with a whole flat of thirty-six tomato plants and, not wanting to waste any, planted every one.

That summer was a busy one for us. My husband was running for a judgeship position that covered two counties. We had a baby in diapers and a five-year-old, and every weekend found us riding in parades, attending political functions, and campaigning until we thought we would drop. August came, and with it the harvest of our backyard vegetable garden. (Do you have any idea how many tomatoes can grow on thirty-six plants?) We were overwhelmed with tomatoes.

One hot, humid afternoon, the Bivinses stopped by. Jenny Bivins was Amber's very best friend, and the girls disappeared upstairs to play. Char Bivins and I sat on the front porch to visit, and our toddlers played on the floor beside us.

"I wish I knew just one more person who could use a tomato," I sighed. "I've given them to everyone I can think of. I just don't have time to can or freeze anything this summer, and the backyard is full of tomatoes rotting on the vine!"

"I'll can them for you," Char replied.

"You have got to be kidding," I responded. Char was well along with expecting her third child and besides that, it was miserably hot and humid.

"I mean it," she said. "It's no big deal."

"Wait a minute, Char. If you want those tomatoes for your *own* use, you can have 'em all. I'll even pick them for you, load your car, and lend my canning jars for a full calendar year. There's no way I'll be using them this year."

So I picked several boxes of tomatoes and loaded them into her car. Then I retrieved four beat-up boxes of canning jars from the basement and packed those in too.

Several weeks went by. I pulled in my driveway one day after a speaking engagement, and sitting on the wide front step in front of our door was a worn, familiar-looking box. *Looks like she didn't need all those jars after all*, I thought, and then with a tinge of guilt added, *Or maybe she did end up canning some of those tomatoes for me.*

I brought the heavy box into the house, only to discover that it wasn't full of tomatoes after all. Oh, there were a few jars of tomatoes, but there was also a cornucopia of beautiful canned goods inside, jars of canned peaches, pears, green beans, pickles, and even a jar of jalapeño peppers! However, what made them extra special were Char's notes. Pieces of paper of various sizes were taped on each jar, and in her own handwriting were verses of Scripture, lines of poetry, or little notes of encouragement.

I called her up.

"Thank you, Char. You made a practical gift so special, and I love you for that."

Just a few weeks later we received word that the Bivinses were being transferred to another city. I'll never forget tucking Amber in bed the first night after hearing the news. Folding her hands tightly together, Amber prayed: "Dear Lord, please be with my friend Jenny when she goes to her new kindergarten and I'm not there. Please help her not to be lonely or afraid. And please, Lord, be with me when I go to my kindergarten and Jenny's not there. I just know I'll cry and cry—I think . . . I'll just start . . . right nowwwwww!"

And together we cried because our friends, the Bivinses, were leaving.

Char, that young mother, never knew the particular days she ministered to me—days when I reached for a jar of her canned goods to enhance the "burnt offering" I was placing before my own family. Rushed days. Frustrating days. Ordinary days when her simple words of encouragement on those jars lifted my spirits and touched my heart.

Friendship. A fair definition is intimacy between individuals that rests on mutual esteem, kindness, or aid. Christian friendship has an added dimension that makes it even more meaningful. It's intimacy resting on mutual esteem, kindness, or aid that's encouraged by Jesus's example, prompted by his presence, and enriched by his essence.

There is a remarkable story about friendship that is vividly recorded for us in Mark 2:1–12. Will you step into the pages of the story with me?

The Paralytic Man's Story

The man was lying face up, staring at the ceiling. He knew every line and irregularity in the beams above him, because this was his spot, his place in the house. And how he hated it.

A fly circled overhead, landing for a moment on the beam directly above him, crawled several inches, and then buzzed off, only to buzz back and land on the man's eyebrow. Irritated, he inhaled and, extending his bottom lip, tried to force air in an upward direction to get rid of the pest. The persistent insect ventured closer to the man's eye. The man shut his eyelids tightly and blew again, straining in his effort to dissuade the fly from trespassing farther. It buzzed off again, circling the room as if taunting him.

Anger surged through him and he laughed bitterly, suddenly picturing himself furious at a fly. *No*, he thought. *It isn't the fly, it's life.* It was frustration with his seemingly worthless existence, with his inability to do the simplest things for himself. Where was his caregiver, anyway? At dinner she would prop him up, feed him like a baby, cajole him to eat a bit more, and mop him up afterward. As much as he depended on that assistance, he despised needing it.

I'm a paralytic. What am I good for? A doorstop? A beggar? Sure, just let me beg, he thought sarcastically. His bitter reverie was interrupted by a commotion at the door, and within seconds, four men rushed into the room where he was resting. They were longtime friends, and his countenance, which had been so dour the moment before, brightened considerably. His welcome held only a touch of his earlier sarcasm.

"Hey, guys! All four of you here at once and out of breath? Where's the fire?"

The man nearest him reached for two poles leaning against the wall in the corner and spoke in an urgent tone.

"Jesus has come! He's teaching in a house here in Capernaum," he said, passing one of the poles to another fellow and then kneeling to push the one he still held through the hemmed opening on one side of his friend's pallet.

"He has made blind people see and has made the lame walk again!" proclaimed the man holding the other pole as he performed the identical task on the opposite side of the pallet. The first fellow spoke again.

"Okay, guys, everybody got a corner? One, two, three, lift! We're taking you to Jesus, buddy, because we believe Jesus can make you well. He works miracles. He changes lives. He can change yours." He paused, and they all waited silently with their friend suspended between them. "Are you ready?"

The paralytic looked from one eager face to another, and an emotion he had not entertained for a long while flickered inside him. Hope! The intensity of their faith that Jesus could heal him was contagious, and his face lit up with an anxious smile.

"I'm ready if you guys are."

Once the friends had maneuvered him out the door, they hurried as fast as their burden would allow. With his heart pounding rapidly in his fragile body, the jostled paralytic unconsciously took in the underside of the tree limbs hanging out over the street. He squinted his eyes against patches of sun that appeared between clusters of leafy foliage. His mind raced faster than the feet of his bearers. He had heard of Jesus—of the lives he had changed. Was it possible that Jesus would take notice of him?

"We're almost there, buddy. It's right around this next corner. You're going to be well again!"

Rounding the corner, the small parade came to an abrupt halt.

"Unbelievable! Look at all the people!" said one of the friends.

"The place is so packed that people are standing in the doorway and at the windows," said another.

They stood motionless for a moment, holding the suspended pallet. Then, with resignation the paralytic spoke. "We're too late, guys. After all your effort to get me here, we just came too late. Sorry I slowed you down."

"Wait!" said the ringleader. "Surely folks will let us in. Let's just try."

They carried the man to the door. "Excuse us, sirs. Is this where Jesus is teaching? Excuse us!"

One man nodded impatiently and immediately turned his attention back inside. The other men in the doorway barely gave them a glance, and none moved an inch to accommodate them. But rather than turning back the way they had come, they lowered their friend to the ground and squatted a moment, both to rest and to figure out what to do next.

"We can't just give up," said one.

"Could we find out where in the house Jesus is standing?" asked another.

The tallest of the group rose to his feet. "Let me give it a try." He headed for an open window where people were pressing over the sill from the outside. Standing behind them, he rose up on his toes and narrowed his eyes, trying to see between their heads and into the dim interior. When he located where Jesus was standing, he turned back to his friends.

"I've spotted him!"

"Good," said the leader with a smile. His eyes twinkled. "See those exterior stairs? Do you guys think we can get our friend here up those stairs and onto the roof?"

They all turned their attention to the narrow stairway against the house that led from the ground level to the flat roof and visually measured the distance and the challenge. Then with grins breaking out on their faces, they nodded.

"Okay. Whoever's in front, you'll have to walk ahead of the pallet and hold it behind you. Keep it as low as possible. The tallest guys should be on the bottom, behind the pallet and lifting it high enough to try to keep him level. Ready? One, two, three, lift!"

If the paralytic had thought the ride up to that point had been an adventure, he hadn't experienced anything yet. He held his breath as his body slipped lower on the pallet and the angle became sharper. Yes, it was precarious, but he couldn't help grinning at the sight of his big, impulsive friends clumsily making their way up those narrow steps with him held between them.

Once they were at the top, they lowered him to the flat roof, off to the side next to some earthenware jugs, and out of their way.

"Okay. About where do you think you saw Jesus?"

The tallest member of the group surveyed the area and walked to a point not far from where they were standing. "Right about here, I'd say."

"All right. There's enough width between the beams. We'll remove the tiles between these two first and then dig through the matting underneath until we get the opening big enough. Let's do it!"

When Jesus returned to Capernaum, the word spread like wildfire that he was there. People came from near and far and packed themselves into the house where he was speaking. The audience he was teaching that day was a formidable one, with Pharisees and teachers of the law, who had come from every village of Galilee and from Judea and Jerusalem.

It was warm in the room, with so many crowded in like they were, and ventilation was limited because of the people blocking the doorways and windows. But, in spite of the stuffiness, the crowd listened attentively to what Jesus said. It was a bit irritating to some when there seemed to be a disturbance outside; but, oddly enough, even when a commotion began right above their heads, no one got up to investigate. Not even the property owner. Jesus continued teaching.

First there was the sound of scraping tiles. Then came the scratching and digging noises. Before long, a small hole appeared in the ceiling, and bits of dirt and dusty particles showered the guests as the matting in the ceiling was torn apart. Several started coughing as they inhaled the dust. Others shielded their eyes from the gritty assault while, at the same time, they strained to see what the commotion was all about.

Jesus stopped speaking and looked at the crowd. Most eyes were focused on the bizarre event happening above their heads. A few were watching him—speculating on how he would deal with the rude interruption.

The opening in the roof was large now. The brilliance of the sun brightened the room below, showcasing dusty particles that still floated in the air. Then for a few moments the brightness was blocked by a pallet of some kind being lowered through the aperture. The pallet was suspended by its four corners, and hands in the room below reached up to steady its descent. As it was lowered into the room, the same audience that wouldn't budge to let one more person in a while earlier shifted and made room for the helpless occupant of the pallet that came to rest at Jesus's feet.

While the audience gaped at the paralytic, Jesus looked up at the paralytic's four friends who were gripping the edge of the crude opening with filthy fingers and raw, scraped knuckles. Their heads were framed by the sunshine behind them. Disheveled hair was plastered to their foreheads, and their faces glistened with sweat. But Jesus saw much more than the outward indications of their determination and fatigue. Their eyes were focused on him, and those same dirty faces radiated their avid expectancy—their profound faith.

At Jesus's feet lay another man. Oblivious to the occupants of the room who stared with morbid curiosity or pity at his atrophied muscles and physical helplessness, the paralytic focused on Jesus. And when Jesus looked at him, he saw so much more than physical disability. He saw the bitter, ugly neediness of the paralytic's heart. And he loved him just as he was.

"Son," Jesus said tenderly, as if they were related, "your sins are forgiven."

For all the unexpected excitement of the day, there were parts of it that had been pretty intimidating for the paralytic. It had been an adventure to be raced through the streets by his impulsive friends and even fun, if a little precarious, for the five of them to manage the stairs to the roof. He could hardly believe it when they started tearing up the surface, but when they finally lowered him through the opening, his heart was thundering. He could hear the shocked reaction of the people in the room and was tempted for a moment to put up the old defenses he always used when he knew people were staring or whispering about him. But then he saw Jesus. And nobody else mattered.

When Jesus looked at him, the man sensed that Jesus could see into his very soul. Shame overwhelmed him for a moment as he was stripped of his self-pity, and he saw his sinful heart with startling clarity. But at the same time, there was such hope and longing in that same heart to know this man Jesus, who somehow seemed to know him already.

Jesus looked him in the eye and said, "Son, your sins are forgiven."

Forgiven! The man felt a joyfulness surging through him, filling him with a peace and happiness he had never before experienced. Wholeness. He felt whole, and it had nothing to do with his physical condition. He was so overwhelmed with what had happened to him that it took a moment for him to notice the strange hush that had come over the room.

Jesus looked up from the precious believer who had just been healed spiritually. The Pharisees and teachers of the law were silent, but their minds were full of glaring criticism. *He's blaspheming! Who can forgive sins but God alone?*

Knowing exactly what they were thinking, Jesus shocked them by voicing their very thoughts and asking, "Why are you even thinking these things? Tell me. Do you think it would be easier for me to tell this man that his sins are forgiven, or to tell him to get up and walk? To prove to you that I, the Son of Man, do have the authority on earth to forgive sins . . ."

Jesus turned to the paralytic and gave him nine simple words of instructions.

"Get up. Take up your mat and go home."

The shock jolted the man, but he didn't hesitate. He immediately leaped to his feet. No one assisted him. No therapists were needed to rehabilitate the wasted muscles. He was not only well, but he was strong; not only standing, but agile. With the gaping crowd staring at him in astonishment, he bent, rolled up his mat, hoisted it over his shoulder, flashed a brilliant smile at Jesus, and ran out the door, yelling, "Praise God! Praise the Lord God! He has made me *whole!*"

The teachers of the law and the Pharisees inside the house were awestruck, and they too began praising God, saying, "We have never seen anything like this!"

And outside? Four friends on the roof cheered loudly and hugged one another with tears of joy streaking down their grubby cheeks. Then they raced down the stairs at breakneck speed to embrace their friend.

Digging Deeper

As I studied this fascinating story, I realized that it had several important elements.

Faith and determination paid off. The friends of the paralytic truly had faith that Jesus could heal their friend, and they were determined to get him to Jesus. The paralytic's disability alone could have been a huge impediment to stop them, but they worked together to bring him to Jesus in spite of it.

I've wondered if they were young men, and I can't help speculating that they were. They were so impulsive! When they got to the house and couldn't get anybody to make room for them (and there definitely were no handicapped parking spots available), shouldn't they have waited until the meeting ended and caught Jesus on his way out? Instead of waiting patiently, however, they brainstormed and came up with the idea of hauling their friend up to the roof. The book on biblical times and culture that I studied explained that the houses often had flat roofs with steps leading up along the exterior of the house. The steps were often narrow and sometimes angled sharply.

Well, if it was gutsy to try to get him to the roof, imagine how outrageous their next action was. They started destroying private property! In Luke's record of this story, it says that they had to move tiles before they could start digging up the matting underneath (Luke 5:19). Isn't it amazing that no one stopped them? When bits of dirt started showering the people below, why didn't the homeowner run outside and yell, "Stop that or I'll call the police!" At least he could have hollered, "Just stop tearing up the place and we'll let you come in!" Why was that outrageous act of vandalism allowed to happen?

Jesus was in control of the entire situation. In both the Mark and Luke versions of this story, it is recorded that Jesus knew the thoughts of the skeptics in the room. Luke's record describes the audience as distinguished educators (teachers of the law) and Pharisees who had come from every village in Galilee and from as far away as Judea and Jerusalem.

Why didn't somebody stop the vandals on the roof? Because Jesus knew exactly what was happening. He kept the audience in place while the large opening was being made right above their heads (which had to have taken some time), because he had a memorable lesson to teach everyone present, from the paralytic, to his friends, to the doubters in the crowd.

Jesus's timing was unexpected, and it emphasized his priorities. He did not immediately heal the paralyzed man. The crowd must have been holding their breath to see what would happen after the man was lowered to the floor, wondering just how good the "show" would get. Of course, we don't know the extent of the man's paralysis. Scripture doesn't say, but because he's flat on his back until the very end of the story, and because of the crowd's amazement when Jesus finally did heal him, I figure that he was very obviously handicapped. Jesus had performed other miracles, but those in attendance are quoted as saying that they were amazed and had never seen anything like it.

How can this story apply to your life?

Don't give up on your friends. The paralytic had one gigantic blessing in his life. He had four friends that truly cared about him, and most importantly, they *believed*. The Scripture says that Jesus "saw their faith" (Mark 2:5). What an incredible example for those of us who may feel like we've come up against a brick wall in our effort to introduce a friend or relative to Jesus. We need to *believe* that God will change their lives, and we must be willing to go out of our way to introduce them to the Savior.

Jesus recognizes our need. Jesus healed the paralytic spiritually. When Jesus looked at the man at his feet, he didn't just see the outward helplessness that was so apparent to the crowd. He saw the man's need for spiritual wholeness as far more important than his physical neediness. If Jesus could read the minds of the skeptics in the room, I figure he could read the soul-cry of the paralytic (and us!), too.

In 1 Samuel 16:7 it says, "Man looks at the outward appearance, but the LORD looks at the heart."

Jesus shows his power in our lives. Jesus dramatically finished his lesson for the day by healing the man physically. No hocus-pocus. No theatrics. The Bible doesn't even say that Jesus touched the man. He simply instructed him to pick up his mat and go home. And the man who miraculously had been made both spiritually and physically whole walked out, praising God and leaving the shocked audience as eyewitnesses to the power of Jesus, the Son of God. Jesus can exhibit this power in your life, as well as in the lives of your friends.

The faith and determination of four friends made all the difference in introducing the paralytic to Jesus Christ. Have you introduced anyone to him lately? Are you willing to overcome obstacles to introduce your friend to Jesus?

I loved my neighbor Sarah. She was everything a good neighbor should be. She brought over cookies when we moved in across the street, she volunteered to babysit my little girl, and she helped me put together a potluck dinner to help others feel welcome in the neighborhood. Sarah was a good person from a wonderful family, and she went to church every Sunday. However, as I got to know her, I wasn't sure if she knew Jesus personally.

So I started praying for Sarah every day. Then I invited her to attend Christian Women's Club with me, knowing she would enjoy the luncheon and the speaker, hoping she would come to understand that it was possible to have a personal relationship with God by inviting his Son, Jesus Christ, into her life. She turned me down. I invited her again and again. Thirteen months in a row, she said a cheerful, "No thanks."

Then my friend Debbie phoned to say, "Jennie, I think that we should have a young moms' Bible study group, that it should be at your house, that you should teach it, and that I should invite people!"

I laughed. "Debbie, that sounds like a lot more work for me than it would be for you, but I'll tell you what. I've been praying for my neighbor for over a year. I'll invite her to come, and if she says yes, I'll do it."

I approached Sarah with no confidence. After all, she was a veteran at turning down my invitations. "Sarah, you wouldn't be interested in coming to my house for a young moms' Bible study group, would you?"

To my shock, she said that she'd like that very much.

We made arrangements to use a church nursery down the street from my house and hired a sitter to watch our children. The women came, and our time together in God's Word was wonderful. Sarah seemed to enjoy the group a lot, but when anyone shared about how they had come to accept Jesus Christ, Sarah was silent.

One afternoon I was on my knees praying, my elbows in the seat of the sofa in my living room. The house was quiet, and as I prayed for Sarah, it occurred to me that the time to talk to her about Christ had come.

But I was afraid. We had such a nice, comfortable relationship. What if I offended her? I prayed for courage and the wisdom to know what to say to her, and then I got up and walked across the street.

She invited me in, but I was so nervous that I wasted twenty minutes talking about nothing. Finally, I awkwardly blurted, "Sarah, I like you for a neighbor so much."

She grinned and responded, "Well, I like you too, Jennie."

I sighed and nodded. "Sarah, I need to ask you a personal question. Would you be offended if I did that?"

She lifted both hands palm-up in midair and grinned again. "Ask me anything!"

Oh, my, I thought. *Here I go.*

"Sarah, you've been coming to our study group for over six weeks now, and you seem to like it a lot. Am I right?"

She nodded.

"Well, some of the rest of us have shared how we came to open our hearts and lives up to Jesus Christ, but you've never said anything. Do you know him, Sarah? Have you ever invited him into your life?"

I figured Sarah would say, "Yes." I mean, she was such a lovely person and a faithful churchgoer. But she slowly shook her head, and tears began to run down her cheeks.

"I've gone to church all my life, Jennie, and I've never even known why. When my kids were born, I just figured it was a good, wholesome place for them, so I kept on going. I've never invited God into my life."

My heart was thundering, but I was so moved by her confession and obvious need that the words came pouring out. "Oh, Sarah, he loves you so much. God sent his Son, Jesus, into the world to be born. He lived a sinless life, Sarah, but he chose to die on the cross to pay for my sin and for yours. He rose from the dead and ascended into heaven. He is there, preparing a place for us to spend eternity with him, but he wants to do so much more."

Taking a deep breath, I continued. "It's simple, Sarah. If we, by faith, believe and invite him into our lives, his Spirit comes to live within us. We will not only be with him in eternity, but we have access to his peace, his joy, his wisdom, and his comfort every day. We can have a personal relationship with God because he becomes our Heavenly Father. It is an awesome and precious gift, Sarah. Would you like to invite him into your life and get to know him, too?"

Sarah's tearful eyes searched my earnest ones for a moment, and then she nodded.

My heart felt like it was bursting. "Sarah, you can just talk to God and tell him you need him. All that's necessary is for you to confess to him that you're a sinner, believe in your heart that Jesus died for you to pay for that sin, and invite him into your life. If you'd like, I could pray first, Sarah. Would you like me to do that?"

She nodded again, wiping a tear from her cheek with one hand.

So two young moms in a living room bowed their hearts before God. I prayed a simple prayer, and Sarah repeated each phrase after I said it.

"Dear God, I need you. I admit I'm a sinner. I have done wrong things. But I do believe that you love me and that you sent your Son, Jesus, to pay for my sins. Please forgive me for my past and make me brand new inside. Thank you for this miracle you are beginning in my life. Help me to grow to know you better every day."

As I finished the prayer and Sarah repeated the last phrase, I figured she was all finished, too. But she wasn't; she added one more line to the prayer, saying it twice. "Oh, God, I've needed you for such a long time. I've needed you for such a long time."

A Passionate Prayer

Dear Heavenly Father, thank you for caring more about the condition of my heart than about my outward appearance. Thank you for the peace and joy that is mine through my faith in your Son, Jesus Christ.

I've been thinking about the one(s) who introduced me to Jesus. Thank you for their persistence and faithful testimony to what a relationship with you is all about. They didn't give up when I made excuses or feigned disinterest. Thank you for using them to draw me to you.

Please help me to recognize the spiritual needs of my own friends. I want to introduce them to you too. Please give me the courage and determination I need to lead them into a life-changing relationship with you.

In the precious name of Jesus, Amen.

The Scripture Reading: Mark 2:1–12

A few days later, when Jesus again entered Capernaum, the people heard that he had come home. So many gathered that there was no room left, not even outside the door, and he preached the word to them. Some men came, bringing to him a paralytic, carried by four of them. Since they could not get him to Jesus because of the crowd, they made an opening in the roof above Jesus and, after digging through it, lowered the mat the paralyzed man was lying on. When Jesus saw their faith, he said to the paralytic, "Son, your sins are forgiven."

Now some of the teachers of the law were sitting there, thinking to themselves, "Why does this fellow talk like that? He's blaspheming! Who can forgive sins but God alone?"

Immediately Jesus knew in his spirit that this was what they were thinking in their hearts, and he said to them, "Why are you thinking these things? Which is easier: to say to the paralytic, 'Your sins are forgiven,' or to say, 'Get up, take your mat and walk'? But that you may know that the Son of Man has authority on earth to forgive sins. . . ." He said to the paralytic, "I tell you, get up, take your mat and go home." He got up, took his mat and walked out in full view of them all. This amazed everyone and they praised God, saying, "We have never seen anything like this!"

Final Note: The story of the paralytic was recorded by Mark, sometime between AD 57 and 63. This story was also reported by Matthew and by Luke. Matthew's record is found in Matthew 9:1–8, and Luke's record is found in Luke 5:17–26. Read all three passages for greater insight into the details of the story. This miraculous healing occurred toward the beginning of Jesus's public ministry, shortly before he chose his twelve apostles.

8

Look Who's Coming to Dinner
A Story about Choices

It was a beautiful summer day, and the new pastor of a small midwestern church was making calls on the elderly in his congregation. Many of the elderly were widows, and their delight at meeting the new pastor and visiting with him was heartwarming. After finishing several calls, he checked his church directory and county map and discovered that there was one more lady who lived in the area whom he could make contact with. He had phoned ahead to set up appointments with all the others but felt it might be all right, just this once, to stop by a house unannounced.

As he approached the house, he noticed that a curtain at one of the front windows moved a bit, and he figured that the owner must have noted his arrival. However, when he rang the bell, no one answered. He tried knocking and then ringing the doorbell once again, all to no avail. So, taking one of his new business cards out of his pocket, he turned it over and wrote a verse on the back side.

143

Here I am! I stand at the door and knock. If anyone hears my voice and opens the door, I will come in and eat with him and he with me.—Revelation 3:20.

Tucking the card between the door and the doorframe, he went back to his car and headed home.

The following Sunday, the pastor stood at the back of the church, greeting his parishioners following the service. Many of the elderly he had called on the week before stopped to express heartfelt gratitude for his visit. A wrinkled old lady with snow-white hair and a twinkle in her eye made her way up to him, aided by the use of an ivory cane. He didn't recognize her as anyone he had met before.

"Hello, Pastor. I'm Myrtle Samuelson from out on Watkins Road."

Resting her weight on the cane with her left hand, she reached out her blue-veined right hand and handed him a small card. "Thanks for stopping by," she said, and with that, she turned and went on her way.

His attention was immediately demanded by the next person in line, so he slipped the card into his pocket. When he got home he pulled out the card, and read only a reference: Genesis 3:10. When he looked it up, he chuckled to read: *I heard your voice in the garden, and I was afraid because I was naked; and I hid myself* (NKJV).[1]

Have you ever wished you had been more prepared for unexpected company? I have, and I found an intriguing story about someone else who must have felt the same way too.

There is a record in the Bible about a woman named Martha who opened her home to Jesus. Her house in Bethany was a place where Christians would often gather, and she lived there with her siblings, a sister named Mary and a brother named Lazarus. Jesus, in his early thirties and on the road in ministry, was a close personal friend to the family.

In Luke 10:38–42 there is a story recorded about one of Jesus's visits to this home. It is a snapshot of an intensely emotional moment in the life of Martha, Jesus's friend and hostess.

Martha's Story

This day had started like any other. Arising at dawn, Martha had prepared a simple meal of curds and bread for herself and her family. After clearing the table, she and Mary lifted large earthenware jars to their shoulders and headed to the village well to draw water. They were greeted warmly by most of the other women at the well, but while Mary lingered to enjoy the conversation, Martha waved a friendly good-bye and headed home.

The village of Bethany was built on the southeast slope of the Mount of Olives, less than two miles east of Jerusalem, and Martha's home was one of the most prominent in the village.[2] As she approached the house, she swept an appreciative glance over the structure, thankful that, although life had not always been easy, she was blessed with her own home and enough financial security to be generous.

Once inside, she collected the wheat flour that had been ground the day before at the millstone and, instructing a servant to collect twigs and grass to aid in lighting the ovens, set to work mixing the household's daily bread. She mixed water with the flour and then reached for some of the previous day's bread dough with yeast in it, kneading it all together. As she worked the dough, occasionally pausing to scrape the gooey substance from between her fingers, her thoughts wandered to Jesus.

Word had it that there had been a recent assassination attempt on his life. Martha sighed and punched the dough. It was beyond her why the religious leaders hated him so much. He fed the hungry and healed the sick. Crowds followed him everywhere. He had done nothing but good, showing compassion to all, and even teaching that people should love their enemies. Perhaps most touching of all to her was the fact that he was a rabbi for women as well as for men. He treated women with respect, and that broke with tradition. Jewish men were taught not even to speak to a woman in public. But Jesus not only spoke to women, he befriended and healed them. He changed their lives.

Covering the dough with a cloth and setting it aside to rise, she rinsed her hands, her thoughts still on Jesus. Ever since he had healed Simon the leper in Bethany, his popularity among the people in her village had expanded. It pleased her that it was known in the community that he and his disciples came to her home for rest and refreshment when he was in the area. His friendship was precious to her, and she was honored to be a small part of his ministry in this practical way. She chuckled a moment, admitting to herself that it wasn't exactly a *small* thing to have Jesus and his entourage come to visit! They were company, all right. Thirteen hungry men and twenty-six extra feet to wash was no small undertaking, but she knew without doubt that Jesus appreciated her effort, and she had made quite a name for herself as a hostess.

As time wore on, Martha's day was filled with productive activity. While Mary worked at the loom weaving a fine cloth, she shaped the bread dough into large, flat disks for baking in the ovens. She was careful to save part of the raw dough for the next day's leavening. Then she instructed her servant to sweep the stone walkway in the courtyard, to grind barley for the next day's bread, and to keep an eye on the baking bread while she went to the village market.

Martha purchased a small oil lamp from one vendor and moved on to buy honey and figs from another. Almost finished with her shopping, she stopped to examine a basket of ripe pomegranates, choosing three to take with her. It was then that she became aware of a small group of Pharisees standing beside the road. They were in deep conversation, and she wondered if they gestured toward her. A feeling of unease crept over her, but she lifted her chin and turned away. It was no crime to be a friend of Jesus, and she would not humor them by acting frightened. However, she found herself hurrying home.

Later that day, with her errands completed, Martha worked with Mary on the mending. Mary, the quieter of the two, listened as Martha told her about the incident at the marketplace.

"I wish Jesus wouldn't have to suffer," responded Mary softly. Looking at her sister, she went on, "It's inevitable, you know."

Missing Mary's point completely, Martha continued, "Those men made me so uncomfortable! I just don't know what this world is coming to!"

They were quite a crew, the disciples following Jesus. There were two sets of brothers: Peter and Andrew, who were fishermen from Galilee, and James and John, the sons of Zebedee, who hailed from Capernaum. There was Thomas, and James, the son of Alphaeus. Philip was from Bethsaida, and Bartholomew from Cana in Galilee. Matthew had been a tax collector in Capernaum before joining the group. Simon the Canaanite had been a Jewish revolutionary who opposed Rome. Then there was Judas Iscariot, who acted as treasurer for the group, and lastly, the warm-hearted Thaddaeus. Traveling with Jesus from town to town as he taught the crowds and healed the sick had been an unexpected calling on their lives that they had passionately responded to. It wasn't an easy vocation, following Jesus Christ. They had left their jobs, homes, and families to heed his call.

And times were more and more perilous with the religious leaders cracking down on them. King Herod had put John the Baptist to death, which had grieved them all, but Jesus's fame was still spreading like wildfire. He had recently amazed both his disciples and a multitude of hungry people who had come to hear him teach. There were five thousand men, plus women and children, who had gathered in one spot, and Jesus had fed them all, using only the lunch of one little boy. It had been astounding! In addition to that miracle, the disciples had been empowered by Christ to heal the sick and to cast out demons from the tormented! Who would ever have dreamed that God would work this power through simple men? No, it wasn't easy to follow Jesus, but they were committed disciples.

After a long day of dealing with people, helping with crowd control, and assisting Jesus, the disciples were on the road, hoping to reach the village of Bethany before nightfall. The thought of the welcome that would await them lightened their hearts and made their stomachs growl.

Andrew dramatically sniffed the air. "I think I can smell Martha's pita bread from here!"

"And her chicken soup!" added Peter.

Laughter erupted from the men, and Matthew responded, "Just so it's not fish! All you two ever fix us is fish!"

As Jesus walked along with the disciples, he smiled at their bantering. His heart was heavy, though, with the magnitude of all they needed to learn before he would be crucified. There was so much they did not yet understand, and time was short.

But the thought of making himself at home in Martha's house and of seeing Mary and Lazarus was heartwarming for him as well. Since he had entered his public ministry well over two years before, he had been on the road constantly, virtually homeless. The welcome that always awaited him in Bethany and the company of the dear friends who lived there were precious to him.

The commotion in the courtyard announced their arrival before they even knocked. When Martha threw open the door, her face lit with surprise and welcome.

"Jesus! Friends! Come in. Come in!" Turning away for a moment, she called, "Mary! Lazarus! We have company!"

The entryway was soon filled with twenty-six more sandals as the men doffed their shoes and warm greetings were exchanged. As they followed Lazarus into the main room, Mary got out a basin with water and clean cloths to begin the ritual of foot washing.

Martha disappeared into the kitchen, her mind racing. *I wish Jesus had sent a runner to give me a little advance warning of his coming!* she thought as she arranged a tray with cups and poured a mixture of wine and honey into each. Glancing out the open kitchen door at the fading daylight, she had another wishful thought. *If only the market was still open!*

She hoped that the arrival of her company hadn't drawn the attention of too many others in the community. She was usually proud to have Jesus in residence, but with the political unrest lately, she knew there were those who would like to do him harm. Hopefully there would be no arrests made at her door this night!

She carried the heavy tray into the room where the men had gathered, noticing that Mary was still making the rounds washing feet. Water was poured over each foot, which was then rubbed with hands and dried with a towel. Accustomed to this ritual, the men had made themselves comfortable, and Jesus began to teach them. Occasionally one would ask a question and a discussion would ensue, with Jesus often illustrating his lessons by telling stories or parables. Wishing she had time to sit and listen herself, Martha headed back to the kitchen.

Taking a quick inventory of the food available for a presentable meal, she felt frustrated that she hadn't made a bigger batch of bread that morning. There were eggs and smoked mutton in the root cellar, along with the pomegranates she had purchased that day. But usually a meal for guests would include three courses arranged on trays and ending with fruit and a sweet dessert. She put a large kettle of water on the fire to boil and began slicing the mutton for soup. Perhaps the neighbor would have extra bread and cheese.

Mary hadn't shown up in the kitchen yet, so Martha slipped out to the house next door. It was customary that if one had guests, neighbors could be counted on to contribute to a meal. But it still galled her a bit to have to ask. Her errand netted two loaves of bread and a pungent block of cheese, wrapped in a thin cloth.

The kitchen was warmer now, and Martha's cheeks flushed as she worked over the meal. Her eyes stung as she chopped onions and garlic to add to the pot, and her resentment flared. Where was Mary? She should be helping with the kitchen detail. Wiping her hands on a towel, Martha headed for the meeting room, her eyes seeking her sister. Of all things! She was sitting on the floor at Jesus's feet, doing nothing but listening! What did she think she was doing? It wasn't even proper for women to sit with men during a meal! Something inside of Martha exploded.

149

Jesus surveyed the listeners in the room as he taught. Looking beyond their varied exteriors, he could see their expectancy, their trust, their hope. But he could also see that his disciples did not yet understand that he had not come to establish an earthly kingdom in their lifetimes. He had come to give his life for the sins of the world, to provide a new life for all who believed, and to establish an eternal kingdom in heaven where they would one day reign with him.

His eyes dropped to the quiet young woman at his feet. Mary was the one exception in the room—the only one who understood why he had come and that he would suffer. Their eyes met, and hers filled with love and sadness, his with affirmation.

An unexpected commotion in the person of Martha burst into the room. "Distraught" was a fitting description for the normally gracious woman. Without waiting for Jesus to complete his lesson, let alone his sentence, she interrupted her honored guest, casting blame on him for her situation.

"Lord, don't you even *care* that my sister has abandoned me to serve you and your men alone? Tell her to get up and help me!"

A shocked silence came over the room. Mary's mouth dropped open at the sight of her angry sister, and she flushed scarlet. The men gaped at Martha for a moment, and then looked away.

Jesus, the Son of God, looked at Martha, his distraught friend, and saw beyond the flushed cheeks, moist upper lip, and watery eyes. Trembling with outrage, she stood challenging whether or not he cared how hard she worked to serve him, when they both knew that he did indeed care very much.

Jesus reached out to gently grasp her hand, and quietly said her name. "Martha." When she did not immediately respond, he took her hand in both of his and repeated her name again. "Martha."

When she finally made eye contact with Jesus, Martha forgot her sister, she forgot her shocked audience, and she had a moment of reckoning like none other in her lifetime.

"You are worried and upset about many things," said the Lord.

Jesus could see into her very soul. While everyone else saw her outer agitation, he understood that her frustration, her nervous tension, her lack of poise and self-control were not just about dinner. Martha saw herself as naked before him, with her pride, her perfectionism, her fear, and her genuine love for him intermingled.

"Anything would do for dinner, Martha," he said kindly. "You see, there is just one thing that's truly important for the people in this house to receive, and that is to understand the vital importance of why I've come. My time is short, Martha. Mary understands that, and she made the right choice. I'm not going to ask her to leave."

How is it possible to feel loved and rebuked at the same time? Martha wondered. For the first time she realized that for Mary the evening had been all about Jesus, while she, Martha, had chosen to turn the focus of the entire night upon herself. She could have singled out Mary quietly, without disrupting the entire teaching session. She hadn't done that, she realized, because she wanted Jesus and everyone else to know how hard she was working. Not one man would have complained if she had simply served bread and cheese. Then she could have sat and listened to Jesus herself. Instead, she had to prove that no one worked harder than Martha. And to elevate herself even higher, she had tried to shame Mary and make her look lazy in front of everyone present. She had impressed them, all right. They would never forget her sharp tongue.

As embarrassing as this encounter with Jesus was, the lesson Martha learned was one that would change her life.

Digging Deeper

While studying this woman from another time and culture, I found myself fascinated by tidbits of information that I gleaned from scholars who studied before me. References to food, the social and religious customs of the time, the political climate, and an understanding of Jesus's constant traveling companions added color and emotion to this unique story.

While telling you about Martha, I wanted to give you a taste of what a typical day in the life of a Jewish woman living at that time might have been like. I also wanted you to get a glimpse of the political and religious discrimination that existed, so you can better understand the tension that the disciples and those close to Jesus lived with on a daily basis.

Before we look at some important lessons we can learn from Martha's story, I'd like to share some answers to questions that popped into my mind as I studied.

Why were Martha and Mary single? While some scholars speculated that Martha may have been a widow, one writer suggested that these women were very likely close to Jesus's own age and pointed out that King Herod had killed all the boy babies in that area after Jesus's birth, so that "there must have been many unmarried women."[3] This insight made me get out a map to see how far Bethany was from Bethlehem, where Jesus was born, and I learned it was only about five or six miles away. Interesting. Whatever the reason was that Martha and Mary had remained single, it is heartwarming to note that Jesus, single and on the road in ministry, took joy in spending time at the home of his single friends.

What was customarily expected when company showed up? Hospitality during Martha's time was far more complicated than it is today. Servants removed the guest's sandals, and once the guest was seated, or reclining, the ritual of foot washing began. This ritual was practical in that people usually walked wherever they traveled, so their feet got filthy on the dirt roads. Many homes had handwoven carpets on the floors and the foot washing protected the rugs.

Lunch often consisted of a flat loaf of bread stuffed with either cheese or olives. Dinner was a greater challenge. "At a formal meal there was a 'starter' of wine diluted with honey to drink. The main dinner . . . was of three courses arranged on trays and often beautifully decorated. Guests ate with their fingers except when soup, eggs, or shellfish were included, in which case they used spoons. . . . Finally there was a dessert of pastry and fruit."[4]

Often, because of the great distances people walked to reach their destination, a visit also required overnight accommodation. It's clear that if Martha intended to impress her guests, her challenge was considerable.

Why did women love, follow, and support Jesus in his ministry? Martha and Mary were not the only women who loved Jesus. Matthew, Mark, and Luke all refer to the fact that many women followed Jesus (Matthew 27:55; Mark 15:41; Luke 8:3; 24:1). Some women are named, while others are not. Luke mentions that women provided for Jesus and his disciples from their own substance. Why?

> Jewish tradition frowned upon women studying with rabbis. Some rabbis actually considered it sinful to teach women the Law. Women were permitted in the synagogues, but custom required them to sit apart from the men. Menstruation made them unclean each month according to the Law (Lev. 15:19). Women were often viewed as the cause of men's sexual sins. To prevent any temptation, Jewish men were instructed not to speak to a woman in public—even to one's wife. And they were never to touch a woman in public.
>
> But not only did Jesus speak to women in public (John 4:27), he dared to take them by the hand (Mark 5:41). . . . And as he tried to help people understand the kingdom of God, he used illustrations that women as well as men could relate to.[5]

Although his acceptance of women most likely offended many Jews, it is no wonder that women followed Jesus. He was the Son of God who healed the sick, fed the hungry, and offered salvation and eternal life to all who would believe. In addition to that, he loved and valued women and children.

How can this story apply to your life?

Exercise your best gifts for God's glory. Without a doubt, Martha was blessed with the gift of hospitality, and she used that gift to honor her Lord on many occasions.

Have you identified what your best gifts are? Are you using them regularly? Do you use them to bring honor to God? Have you considered opening your home for Jesus's sake? That might mean inviting a lonely co-worker home for dinner or extending hospitality to your neighbors and making your faith visible. It might mean offering your home or cottage as a place of refreshment for your pastor and his family or opening your home for a Bible study. Has the youth group been invited to enjoy your backyard? Most importantly, have you ever shared Christ with a visitor?

I remember staring out the back door of my house when I was a busy young mom and resenting that our backyard was always full of children. Why did I have to buy all the Band-Aids and make all the Kool-Aid? I had a home business and was so busy, but there was a constant trail of kids heading for my bathroom. Children were everywhere: in the tree house, on the swing set, splashing in the kiddie pool. There were girls dressing dolls and boys chasing each other with Nerf guns. I was tired of it.

Then one day the phone rang. It was Michael Spikes, a voice from the past. Michael had been a junior high kid in our youth group at the Main Post Chapel when Graydon was in the military ten years before. We had introduced Michael to Jesus, and we loved him. But to be honest, he hung out at our house so much that sometimes we wished he would stay home a little more often. His call, however, was precious to me. He had grown up and was a young military officer in his own right, stationed in Washington DC. His message was simple and heartfelt.

"I've wanted to thank you and Graydon for years for always making room for me in your lives while we were all at Ft. Polk. I never told you that my parents divorced that last year you were stationed there. My home was hell on earth, but I'd get on my bike and head for your house and everything would be okay. You have no idea how much I needed your love and the reminder that God loved me too."

I had tears in my eyes when I hung up the phone. I looked out my back door with new eyes, realizing that God had given me a mission field, and it was in my own backyard. The best gift I could give to God was to open my heart to the little ones that came and introduce them to him.

Don't neglect time at Jesus's feet. Jesus never rebuked Martha for being a hard worker, but he did stress that Mary had made the wiser choice. He said, "You are upset and worried about many things. . . ."

I'm so glad Jesus didn't say, "You are so worried and upset about *dinner!*" My research suggests that perhaps Martha was frustrated because she wasn't listening to Jesus too, knowing in her heart that she should have been there. Randy Alcorn, in an article entitled "Can't You See That I'm Busy?" comments on the choices that were made that night. "Jesus stresses the issue of Mary's choice. Yet Martha also had a choice, even though she probably thought her hands were tied. 'I have to do this work,' she rationalized. 'It's not a matter of preference, but necessity.' How many times do we use this as an excuse to neglect time with God?"[6]

The word "worried" comes from a Greek word for "pieces" and "mind." Martha had a divided mind. She was distracted.

I can't tell you how many times I've been so busy with impromptu temptations or urgent needs around me that I've neglected doing the truly important things I had meant to accomplish. So often I've put aside my Bible to answer the phone or go to an appointment and have never made it back to God's love letter to me. I've been easily distracted from spending time at his feet.

I've wondered too if, for a little while, Martha forgot that she was entertaining the Son of God. Jesus treated her with such loving familiarity and traveled with such a common bunch of men that perhaps she lost sight of the fact that her guest was the Christ.

Learn from your mistakes. Isn't it interesting that Martha was so distracted with her complaint that Jesus had to call her name twice before he really had her attention? Only one other time during his earthly ministry did Jesus call someone's name twice (Simon in Luke 22:31).

However, once he had her attention, she saw her complaint for what it was—a plea for attention. "Lord, I don't feel important enough right now; please say something so everybody in the room will know I'm important."

Her hospitality that evening had become about her instead of honoring him. Several of the scholars I studied were of the opinion that Martha's home was a wealthy one. It was large enough to accommodate many guests and was well known in the village. The costly gift that her sister Mary gave to Jesus in John 11 is additional evidence of their wealth. If that was the case, Martha would have had a servant or several servants to assist her in the kitchen, and her complaint was more petty than we might realize at first glance.

Whatever the case, Jesus saw right through her. He said, "You are worried and upset about *many* things."

The scholar Matthew Henry suggests that Martha was a brave and loyal woman because she welcomed Jesus into her home even though "at this time it had grown dangerous to entertain him, especially so near Jerusalem."[7] I believe that Martha had all kinds of things on her mind and the meal was merely the straw that broke the camel's back!

Jesus often spoke using metaphors and word pictures. When he said, "only one thing is needed," some suggest he meant that only one item of food was needed. Perhaps this is true, but I believe the "one thing" he was referring to was the need for those present to understand why he had come to earth. Mary, who some time later anointed him with costly perfume normally used for burial, understood. There was no way Jesus would ask her to leave.

The good news is that the gentle rebuke from Jesus taught Martha an important lesson about setting priorities and recognizing who Jesus really was. In John 11:17–27 Martha had a rare one-on-one counseling session with Jesus, which ended with her passionate statement of faith: "Yes, Lord, I believe that you are the Christ, the Son of God, who was to come into the world." It was a heartfelt confession of faith that is one of the most beautiful recorded in Scripture.

At one time she had been more concerned with making the right impression. She finally recognized the value of the relationship with God that Jesus was offering her and the others in her home.

Have you considered opening your home in a way that would honor God and allow you to represent him to others? The important things are not how grand your home is or how impressive the meals you serve are. Instead, impress your guests with your genuine friendship, your sincere interest in their welfare, and your attitude that reflects your relationship to God. Who knows? One day, you may have the opportunity to introduce them to the Savior.

Looking back, I realize that I've had a lot in common with Martha, and I too had some important lessons to learn about pride and how it is more important to represent my Savior than to impress others with who I am or where I live.

We were house hunting from a distance. After almost four years in the military, my husband and I were ready to come "home" to Michigan, become part of a community, and establish Graydon's law practice.

My sister Carol was thrilled that we were considering Fremont, the lovely small town where she and her husband lived. Knowing we loved antiques, she sent us a picture of an old Victorian house on Maple Street that happened to be for sale. I fell in love with the house in the picture, and I started dreaming that it would be mine. I also started bargaining . . . with God.

"Dear Lord," I prayed, "if you'll give me that house on Maple Street, I'll make it an open home for you. I'll entertain missionaries and the pastor and his family. The church youth group can come, and the women's missionary circles can meet there too." To further press my advantage with God, I misquoted Scripture to him.

"Lord, in Psalm 37 you've told me that you'll give me the desires of my heart, and Lord, that house on Maple Street is just exactly what I desire."

I also made my husband's life miserable. It was his dream to set up his own private law practice, but I wanted no such thing. It was too risky! We'd sacrificed enough during law school. I wanted security and a steady paycheck.

To appease me, he wrote letters to three attorneys, chosen at random from the Fremont phone directory. I typed those letters, and they didn't please me much. In essence, they said:

> Dear Sir:
>
> Do you have an opening in your office? If not, I look forward to meeting you when I arrive in Fremont.
>
> Sincerely yours,
> Graydon W. Dimkoff

Well, the letters were a bit more eloquent than that, but that's about all they said. It didn't sound to me like he wanted a job at all! Two of the attorneys responded, saying that they were not planning to expand their offices. The third, Mr. Harry Reber, didn't respond.

During my spring break from teaching, we made a quick trip to Fremont to find both a home and an office for Graydon's practice. The first place we stopped was the old house on Maple Street. I loved it! My heart beat fast as we stepped onto the big enclosed porch and then walked through the large rooms. I knew the house was where I was supposed to live.

Then we started searching for office space to rent. There was none.

In a quandary as to what to do, we strolled through the business district until we came to an abandoned building. It was in miserable shape, but the location was perfect. Rubbing some grime off the cracked front window with a tissue, we peered inside at the cavernous interior.

"This would be great!" Graydon enthused. "Maybe the owner would remodel just the front for my office space."

We made inquiries about the building and were told to contact an attorney named Harry Reber. That name sounded a little *too* familiar. Mr. Reber was the attorney who hadn't replied!

I remember walking into Harry's office; it smelled like leather and old books. It smelled established. I found myself wondering how long it would be before my husband's office smelled like that. Harry Reber picked up a document from his desk and studied it for a moment.

"That building isn't for rent, but it's for sale," he said. "It's been wrapped up in trust since the owner died three years ago, and it's the last piece of property to be disposed of. If you're interested in buying, I can help you. If not, I can't. By the way," he added, "did you know there is a very large apartment on the second floor of that building?"

My mind was racing. We weren't interested in buying the building. We wanted to *buy* the house on Maple Street and *rent* office space. I looked at my husband, and to my dismay, I realized that the wheels in his head were moving in an entirely different direction. He nodded to the attorney, asking, "Can we take a look?" I knew what he was thinking: *How convenient. We could live upstairs and work downstairs!*

My thoughts, however, were riotous. *Oh, no you don't, Graydon. I am the newest attorney's wife in this town, and I will not live in a grubby old storefront apartment! I sacrificed with you in law school, and I taught school so we could save every penny I made to put down on a house. Don't you dare ask me to live in a storefront apartment!*

God worked a miracle in a prideful young woman's heart as we crossed the street and put the key into the rusty lock.

We climbed thirty-two dusty stairs, and I didn't even notice the furnace next to the front door or that there were not enough electrical outlets or heating vents. Or that the plaster had fallen from the ceiling in four of the rooms, and the wall colors were atrocious. I loved the place! I saw oak floors and skylights. There were high ceilings, a large kitchen, and a formal dining room. There were three bedrooms and a claw-foot bathtub. With a little work, it would be *perfect*.

159

We bought the building and moved in that summer. Every penny we had saved went into remodeling the first floor into office space, and we rented out two offices to help pay the mortgage. We also plastered and painted upstairs, nicknaming the apartment "The Penthouse." As the moving van pulled away, we stood in the beautiful old dining room and prayed.

"Lord, in your wisdom you have allowed us to buy this building. We'll entertain the missionaries and the pastor's family. The church youth group can come, and any of the ladies' missionary society that can make it up the stairs are welcome. We're giving it back to you. We're trusting you for the clients who will walk through the door downstairs and for the relationships that will be made in this community. Help us to represent you well in this place."

Three years later I was sitting alone in the lobby of the office. Graydon was in court, and I found myself looking around the spacious lobby at the tangible evidence of God's blessing. After nine years of marriage, we were happily anticipating the birth of our first child. Overwhelmed with God's goodness to us, I leaned back in my chair, closed my eyes, and prayed.

"Father, you are so good and so wise. Thank you for this wonderful old building, for the apartment, and for blessing Graydon's practice. Thank you for not bowing to my will when I was dictating my desires to you. We love this place, and we are so grateful for it."

When I opened my eyes, I was surprised to see the owner of the house on Maple Street stepping inside the door. I hadn't seen Mrs. Longnecker for quite some time, but I had heard that her husband had passed away and that she had taken her home off the market.

"Jennie," she said, "I've considered selling my house again, and just as I was walking down the street, it occurred to me how much you young folks had loved the place when you looked at it three years ago. If you're still interested, I won't list it with a realtor, and Graydon could do the legal work, so the price would be even less than it was before. Why don't you talk it over and let me know what you decide."

With a wave, she was gone, and I sat in stunned silence. The verse I had misquoted to the Lord three years ago came clearly to my mind: "Delight yourself in the LORD and he will give you the desires of your heart" (Psalm 37:4). I realized that from the very moment I had sincerely delighted in what the Lord had done, in walked my heart's desire.

A few weeks later, the church youth group moved us. It was quite a job, considering everything from kitty litter to a baby grand piano had to be moved down thirty-two stairs onto Main Street! And it was not without some regret that we left "The Penthouse" to live in the home where we would raise our family.

That night we stood on the front porch of our new house, amid mountains of boxes and household goods, and prayed.

"Oh, Father, thank you for giving us this place in your perfect timing and not our own. Right now, we give it back to you. The youth group's been here already, but you can be sure they'll be back. We'll have the missionaries, the pastor, and the women's groups, too. But Lord, we want to use it for much more than that. We want to be a lighthouse in this neighborhood. We choose to invite *you* to live here with us and to share you with those who spend time here with us."

A Passionate Prayer

Dear Heavenly Father, I squirm with discomfort at the story of Martha, because she reminds me so much of myself. Thank you for her example of an open heart and open home. And thank you for dealing with her in love when she got her priorities messed up.

Father, help me to listen. Make me sensitive to your whisper in my heart as I read your Word. I don't want to miss what you have for me because I am distracted by other things.

Lord, I want to give my best to you. Not for show, not for points, not for fame, but because I love you. Will you encourage me to do that when the "stuff" of life crowds in and tempts me to get offtrack? I desire to use my home as a place where others will see Jesus. Make me aware of opportunities I can take to reach out in love to those around me.

In the precious name of Jesus, Amen.

The Scripture Reading: Luke 10:38–42

As Jesus and his disciples were on their way, he came to a village where a woman named Martha opened her home to him. She had a sister called Mary, who sat at the Lord's feet listening to what he said. But Martha was distracted by all the preparations that had to be made. She came to him and asked, "Lord, don't you care that my sister has left me to do the work by myself? Tell her to help me!"

"Martha, Martha," the Lord answered, "you are worried and upset about many things, but only one thing is needed. Mary has chosen what is better, and it will not be taken away from her."

Final Note: This story was recorded by Luke, a cultured and educated Gentile, in approximately AD 70. Luke was a physician by trade who later became an evangelist, historian, and author of about one-fourth of the New Testament. He is credited with writing both the book of Luke, in which he records all that Jesus "began to do and teach" (Acts 1:1), and the book of Acts, which details the history of the early church.

9

"You're Late, God! Where Were You When I Needed You?"
A Story about God's Timing

At age eighty-six, Pastor William Carmichael was dying. The call came from the church office, and with heavy hearts my daughter and I went to the hospital for one last visit. As we entered his room, his wife hugged us and warned that he might not even know we were there. As Amber stayed back to talk to Lillian, I turned to the bed. My throat tightened at the sight of his frail body laboring for breath. Taking one of his fragile, blue-veined hands in mine, I leaned over to say, "It's Jennie, Pastor Carmichael. I love you. Thank you for the example you've been to me and to my family, and to so many others. I realize that you're going to see Jesus before I will, and that makes me just a little jealous."

His fingers tightened around mine for just a moment, and I knew he had heard me. Later that night, Pastor Carmichael closed his earthly eyes and opened them in heaven to see Jesus.

William Carmichael was from Scotland, and his wife, Lillian, was from England. They met and married in Muskegon, Michigan, where William worked in a foundry. Their lives were radically changed the day they accepted an invitation by a coworker to dinner and a church service. That night they heard the gospel story of Jesus Christ for the first time, and they both accepted him as their Savior. Bill enrolled in Bible college, and their commitment to Christ eventually took them to Ghana, West Africa, where they worked selflessly for twenty-four years, leading many to Jesus Christ.

In their so-called retirement, they moved to Fremont, Michigan, and tirelessly continued to serve the Lord. They were a much-loved part of our church family, but their most vital ministry was calling on the shut-ins in the hospital or nursing homes. Both Pastor Carmichael and Lillian were small of stature but full of spiritual energy. They didn't drive but instead walked the considerable distance from their apartment to church, the hospital, and the nursing homes, daily. Then Pastor Carmichael was struck with cancer. He battled with the disease and then was blessed with a reprieve as it went into remission. As soon as he was on his feet, he was out walking again.

I lived kitty-corner from the local hospital and looked up one day from weeding my front flower beds to see the Carmichaels briskly walking toward the hospital. I was delighted to see him up and about and, with a wave, called out, "Pastor Carmichael! How are you doing?"

Without even slowing his purposeful gait, he waved back and called out to me in his musical Scottish brogue, "Hello, Jennie. The Lord has raised me up to serve him for another day!"

Although tears were shed at his funeral, it was a joyous occasion with music and singing. For those of us who remembered his life and celebrated his homegoing to heaven, it was a wonderful funeral.

A *wonderful* funeral? Does that sound like a misnomer? In John 11:1–45 there's another story about a wonderful funeral, although those who grieved had no idea that the day would end in rejoicing.

Lazarus's Story

Martha stepped into the dimly lit room, carrying fresh linens for Lazarus's bed.

"Is he any better, Mary?"

Her sister looked up from tending the inert form of their brother, her anxiety written plainly on her face.

"No. If anything, he's worse. Oh, Martha, I'm afraid! If only Jesus were here! I know he would make Lazarus well!"

Dropping the bedding on a stool, Martha moved to the bedside. The pallor of her brother wrenched at her heart. "We must send word to Jesus."

She turned to Mary, and they looked solemnly at each other for a moment.

"It could be dangerous for him to come back, but we must send word to him," she repeated. "Surely he will come."

Jesus had left Jerusalem after attending the winter Feast of Dedication. While in the temple there, he had been surrounded by angry Jewish leaders who badgered him with questions and accusations of blasphemy. Circling around him, they had taken stones to kill him. Well aware that this was not the appointed time for his death, Jesus escaped from their grasp and left town with his disciples. They crossed the Jordan River and retreated to the place where John had baptized many and where Jesus himself had first begun his public ministry.

One day a messenger came with urgent news from Bethany. Lazarus, Jesus's dear friend, was gravely ill.

Alarmed at the news, the disciples, who also cared for Lazarus and his two sisters, were relieved when Jesus said, "This sickness will not end in death. No, it is for God's glory so that I may be glorified through it."

Not understanding the significance of Jesus's statement, the disciples were not only relieved that their friend would get well, they were grateful that they wouldn't need to risk their necks by following Jesus back to Bethany, which was within two miles of Jerusalem and in hostile territory.

But then, two days later, Jesus startled his disciples by saying, "Let's go back to Judea."

They were incredulous! "But Jesus," they said, "a short while ago the Jews tried to kill you, and yet you want to go back there?"

Knowing that Lazarus had died while he had waited, Jesus said, "Our friend Lazarus has fallen asleep, but I'm going there to wake him up."

"No problem then, Lord. If he's sleeping, he'll be better in no time." Nodding and concurring with one another, they were quite satisfied to stay where they were.

"Lazarus is dead."

What? Every eye focused on Jesus as he sighed and continued. "And for your sake I'm glad I wasn't there, so that you may believe."

Believe? Of course they believed. Wait a minute. Believe what? They looked at one another in confusion.

Jesus stood. "Let's go to him."

The disciples sat dumbfounded for a minute before Thomas stood, shrugged with resignation, and said, "Come on. We might as well go and die with him."

So the disciples got up, but it was with some reluctance that they left to journey back to Bethany.

The funeral proceedings were still in full swing as they approached the town. The village was crowded with Jews who had traveled from Jerusalem to comfort and grieve with Mary and Martha over the loss of their brother, who had been laid in the burial tomb four days earlier.

Upon his arrival, Jesus did not present himself publicly, but rather sent word to Martha that he had come and then waited a short distance away, outside the village.

With her head pounding with grief and disappointment, Martha stepped outside the back door to escape the throng of people for a moment. But she couldn't help but think of the events of the past week that would forever be etched on her mind. Lazarus, with his final breath, asking for Jesus, and both she and Mary so sure he would show up and change their sorrow into joy. Why hadn't he come? The question brought up an unwanted sob, and she struggled for control.

Jesus had healed strangers, for heaven's sake! He loved their family! They had loved him back! They had given of themselves for his ministry and had opened their home over and over for his use. Why, why, why hadn't he come?

"Psssst. Martha!" The hoarse whisper caught her off guard, and as she turned toward the sound she was shocked to see one of the disciples beckoning her toward the stone wall near her garden.

"Jesus is here. He's not far away. Can you follow me now, without drawing the attention of the others? He wants to see you."

Martha nodded, headed quickly for the back gate, and followed the disciple to the garden where Jesus waited. Her heart was filled with disillusionment. She had believed with her whole heart that Jesus would heal Lazarus, but he had come too late! Her Lord had disappointed her.

Waiting in the shade, Jesus saw Martha approach. Her eyes were red and swollen, and her voice broke as she blurted, "Lord, if you had been here, my brother would not have died." Then, as she looked into his eyes, hope flickered within her and she said, "But I know that even now, God will give you whatever you ask."

Jesus touched her arm and said gently, "Your brother will rise again."

Snuffing her nose and dabbing her eyes with a piece of cloth, Martha slipped back into her practical self and dutifully answered, "I know he will rise again in the resurrection at the last day." Yes, they would one day be in heaven together. But that thought didn't take away the pain.

"Martha." Jesus captured both her elbow and her attention, saying earnestly, "I am the resurrection and the life. Whoever believes in me will live, even though he dies; and whoever lives and believes in me will never die. Do you believe this?"

As she listened and looked into his eyes, a peace she did not understand came over her. "Yes, Lord, I believe that you are the Christ, the Son of God, who has come into the world."

Nodding to her with a gentle smile, Jesus reached to squeeze her hands. "Will you go and tell Mary I'm here?"

"Yes, Lord."

Martha turned and hurried back to the house, where Mary was surrounded by mourners. Calling her aside, Martha whispered, "Jesus is here and is asking for you. Can you go to him?"

"Of course!" Mary, pale and strained, left the house and ran to the place where Jesus waited. The mourners noticed her rush away, and thinking that she was headed to the tomb to mourn, they followed her.

As Mary came toward Jesus, he read the grief and disillusionment on her precious face and groaned within his spirit. She fell at his feet, weeping, and cried out, "Lord, if you had been here, my brother would not have died!"

Even Mary misunderstood his delay. Jesus looked from her bent head and her shoulders bowed with grief to the weeping mourners around her. Covering his own face with his hands, the Son of God wept.

The Jews who had come to mourn with Mary and Martha were not all believers in Jesus Christ. When the news of Lazarus's death had spread, mourners rallied both out of pity and custom, but also curiosity. How would Mary and Martha react to this devastating loss? Would Jesus dare to enter Judea for the funeral when he was well aware that the Sanhedrin wanted to arrest him?

As the crowd followed Mary to the garden, the object of their curiosity stood before them. Mary threw herself at Jesus's feet and voiced her disappointment at his tardiness. And upon seeing her weep, Jesus wept himself!

"Look how he loved Lazarus," the crowd murmured to one another. But others weren't moved in the least by the grief around them and tried to stir up trouble by saying critically, "If he could open the eyes of a man blind from birth, couldn't he have kept Lazarus from dying?"

But Jesus ignored all this. "Where have you laid him?" he asked Mary. The people stepped aside, and those close to Mary said, "Come and see, Lord. We will take you to the tomb."

Still deeply moved, Jesus followed the procession to the burial cave, which had a stone placed over the entrance. Martha was there now, and the crowd had grown larger as news of Jesus's arrival had spread.

"Take away the stone," said Jesus.

There was a shocked silence before Martha spoke up. "Lord! He has been in the tomb for four days already. By now there will be a foul odor!"

"Didn't I tell you that if you believed, you would see the glory of God?"

"Yes, Lord." Martha's breath caught in her throat as she remembered who he was. Whatever happened would bring glory to God. She believed it would be so. Turning, she nodded to several men near her, and the stone was rolled away. The crowd watched in stunned silence.

Jesus prayed and then called out in a loud voice, "Lazarus, come out!"

Shocked exclamations erupted as Lazarus, with linen strips wrapped around his body, hands, and feet, hobbled out of the tomb! Men and women alike cried out. Some shrank back in fear, and others fainted.

"Release him from the graveclothes," instructed Jesus. "Free him."

Martha and Mary, incredulous for a moment, sprang into action, aided by some of the same dear friends who had helped them fold linen and spices around Lazarus's once-lifeless body. Removing the facial cloth, they feasted their eyes on their brother's precious face, and the three of them wept for joy. Lazarus was healthy and vigorous once more!

And Jesus, the Son of God, had proven that he was the Master—even over death. They would never doubt him again.

Digging Deeper

In their grief-stricken disappointment at Jesus's seeming-late arrival, Martha and Mary didn't realize what God had in store for them. Jesus had *allowed* the tragic death of Lazarus in order to demonstrate that he was "the resurrection and the life," before he himself would die and rise again. Plus, as a result of this difficult experience in Martha's and Mary's lives, many came to believe in Christ. He had *entrusted* this pain to them, asking them to believe in him. They would forever go down in history as principals in the last and greatest miracle of Jesus's public ministry.

As I studied the story of Lazarus's death and resurrection, my research answered several obvious questions I had about the story.

Why did the Jewish leaders hate Jesus? Because he was a threat to both their religious influence and their political power under the Roman government.

There were two major Jewish religious groups, the Pharisees and the Sadducees. These two groups joined forces to seek an end to Jesus's life and popularity.

The Pharisees were legalists and were considered "doctors" of the Law of Moses. They were fanatic about rabbinic tradition, and Jesus was definitely not a traditional rabbi! Some of them even refused to eat with non-Pharisees for fear of contamination, while Jesus ate with, touched, and befriended sinners.

The Sadducees were mostly urban aristocrats from Jerusalem and other areas of Judea. They denied life after death, among other things that Jesus taught. Many served on the Sanhedrin, or high council, which was the Jews' Supreme Court. Caiaphas, a Sadducee, served as the high priest and, as such, was the religious power broker during this time in history. *The Word in Life Study Bible* says that "he feared lest the slightest civil disorder would mobilize Roman troops and lead to the nation's downfall. So when Jesus came, drawing the attention of vast numbers of people and performing astounding miracles, especially the raising of Lazarus, Caiaphas determined that He would have to be destroyed."[1]

What were the funeral customs of the time? The Jewish people did not embalm their dead, and because of the hot climate, bodies decomposed rapidly. Burial took place as soon as possible—always within twenty-four hours and usually within just a few hours of death. The job of preparing the body was performed by women, who bathed the corpse, scented it with perfumed oils and spices, and then either dressed the body in the person's own clothing or wrapped it in specially prepared sheets and strips of linen. The body was immediately taken to the tomb, where it was placed on a shelf. The tomb was then sealed tightly with a large stone or slab. "Relatives, friends, and professional mourners (see Matt. 9:23) formed a procession, and anyone meeting it was obliged to show honor to the deceased and the relatives by joining. A eulogy was often delivered at the grave site."[2]

It is interesting to note that when Jesus arrived four days after Lazarus was interred, mourners from Jerusalem still lingered. This may indicate the popularity or prominence of Lazarus's family, or perhaps some of the crowd lingered to see if Jesus would show up.

Why did Jesus wait to come to the aid of his friends? It was *not* because he was afraid of the Jewish leaders who sought to kill him. Although his time on earth was drawing to a close, he knew it was not quite time for his death. "Only a few weeks remained for him to train these people who would be left to carry his name, 'Christians.'"[3] He had an important lesson to teach his followers through this incident.

What if he had come to their aid immediately? Mary, Martha, and Lazarus would have been relieved and grateful. The disciples might have patted him on the shoulder and said, "Way to go, Jesus! Praise the Lord—it's business, or rather, ministry as usual!"

No. He wanted to demonstrate that as the Son of God he was triumphant over death, to increase the faith of those who followed him, and to comfort them and give them hope after his own crucifixion and death. He was also well aware that this demonstration of power would trigger the Sanhedrin to lay the groundwork for his arrest.

Why did Jesus weep? It was not because he grieved over Lazarus's death like the other mourners. He knew he would raise Lazarus from the dead.

There are two schools of thought on this issue.

1. He was filled with compassion over the obvious grief of Mary and the others. We are well aware that he was a man of compassion.
2. He anguished over the unbelief around him.

As I studied the story, I came to the conclusion that it may have been a combination of the two. He loved Martha and Mary, and I am sure he was moved by their grief. It is interesting to me, however, that he didn't break down until he was confronted by the weeping Mary. Although Martha had confronted Jesus with the same accusation, "Lord, if you had been here, my brother would not have died," she still expressed a flicker of faith when she said, "I know that even now God will give you whatever you ask" (John 11:21–22).

When Mary fell at his feet crying out the same accusation, she did *not* express that same flicker of faith. And she had been the one who sat as a disciple at Jesus's feet, drinking in his words.

Did her lack of faith regarding Lazarus's death break Jesus's heart?

Regardless of the cause of his tears, the resurrection of Lazarus profoundly affected both Martha and Mary. At the banquet given in Jesus's honor in John 12:1–11 we see the last snapshots of both women. Martha is once again serving, joyfully exercising her gift of hospitality for her Lord. And Mary is once again at Jesus's feet. Exhibiting remarkable spiritual insight that even his disciples lacked, she will forever be remembered for tenderly anointing Jesus with precious oil as a prelude to his own inevitable burial.

How can this story apply to your life?

Run to the Savior. In spite of their disillusionment, both Martha and Mary went to Jesus and told him exactly what they were feeling. First Peter 5:7 says to "cast all your anxiety on him because he cares for you." Being the pictorial thinker that I am, I figure that means I can *throw* my cares on him. I can *unload* my heartache on him. I can *cry out* my frustration to him. He cares for me. He loves me, and he can handle it. Furthermore, he has a plan that I can't make out yet, and he wants me to trust him to turn my sorrow into joy.

Keep the faith and count your blessings. Martha hung in there by a thread when she met Jesus and first confronted him with her "Lord, if only" cry. The scholar Matthew Henry said that "her faith was true, but weak as a bruised reed."[4] Then at the grave site when Jesus ordered the stone to be rolled away, she forgot her faith. She thought of the horror of Lazarus's decaying body rather than trusting that Jesus knew what he was doing.

Dee Brestin and Kathy Troccoli, in their wonderful book *Falling in Love with Jesus*, have this to say about dealing with disappointments in our lives: "It is easy to say, intellectually, that Jesus is good, that He cares for us, and that He will do what is best in our lives. It is another thing for these truths to get to the heart. . . . How can we possibly get to this point? One of the things God tells us is to look back in the past and see how He was faithful in the lives of other believers, and in our own lives."[5]

In another passage in the book, Kathy says, "Do we still question God? Do I still have days when lifting my head from the pillow feels like an impossible chore? Absolutely. We're trapped in these bodies and we will deal with these things until we see Him face to face. Until then, we must cling desperately to the One who is crazy about us, to the One who has promised us wholeness, to the One who has promised to never let us go."[6]

Has it ever occurred to you that God may take away all other visible means of support so that we learn to count on his trustworthiness?

Embrace the "waiting room." What? Am I joking? When things are desperate and God doesn't seem to be meeting my expectations, I'm supposed to appreciate the "down time"? Carol Kent, in her book *Secret Longings of the Heart,* encourages us not to lose hope when the reality of life falls short of our expectations. "The relinquishment of our unfulfilled expectations has the surprising potential of freeing us to experience greater intimacy with God. It's an act of trusting Him when we cannot see a positive outcome."[7]

To "relinquish" our expectations is to abandon them, to get our hands off our plans, in order to allow God to work in our lives as he desires.

Hindsight was a blessing to Martha and Mary in this story. They had not embraced the waiting room but soon learned that God's timing had an awesome purpose that would shatter their disillusionment, bring glory to God, and greatly increase their own faith.

God loves us so much that he is far more interested in our development than he is in our comfort. Hindsight is a wonderful thing. Looking back we often realize that painful disappointments were maturing, character-building stepping-stones that God used to prepare us for his plan for our lives. These difficult experiences can also comfort us with the fact that although our timing may not be the same as God's, he loves us and cares about our deepest desires. He wants us to wait, to stand back and witness the power of the Lord.

Disappointment with God is a common ailment among many of us. When we think he should be responding to our prayers in a particular way, it is sometimes hard to understand why he isn't quick to give us the answer we seek. Like Martha and Mary, we don't realize all that he desires to accomplish in our lives if we put our faith and trust in him.

Back in 1976, if anyone had asked my young attorney husband what his long-term career ideal would be, he would have said, "I'd like to be a probate court judge and work with kids and families. It would be a ministry as well as a job."

Eight years later an opportunity to run for a district court judgeship presented itself. The court docket was behind schedule, and Graydon was approached by several community leaders about running against the incumbent judge. It wasn't the position he had longed for, but after praying about it and seeking wise counsel, he said yes.

That began a season of intense campaigning and personal and financial sacrifice for both of us. We put together an awesome committee, marched in parades, shook countless hands, sent out bulk mailings, wrote newspaper ads, and prayed. We were exhausted but confident, because we knew we were following God's direction, and therefore we would win. Right? Wrong.

Graydon lost the election by just 4 percent of the vote. It was devastating. Emotionally, physically, financially, and spiritually draining. But Graydon recovered more quickly than I did. He didn't slam doors, yell at the kids, or kick the cat. He just dug back into his practice and continued his community service and church commitments. I struggled with the loss, however. Had we misread God's will? Surely he wouldn't have had us go through such an extreme effort, only to lose!

Eleven years later in 1995, another unique opportunity presented itself. The very judge that Graydon had challenged was retiring before his term of office was completed, and the governor of Michigan would appoint the new district court judge. After conferring with several county leaders and praying about this opportunity, we decided that Graydon should seek the appointment. Since he had already run for the position and only lost by a tiny percentage of the vote, it seemed reasonable that he would be a good candidate. Graydon sought the endorsements of county and state leaders and launched an endorsement campaign that sent hundreds of personal letters from Newaygo County voters to the governor's office.

The appointment process was complicated, and we gingerly felt our way through it. We filled out detailed application forms, making ourselves an open book regarding family, finances, community activities, and political life. A formidable interview with the state bar of Michigan determined the eligibility of the candidates. Finally, the two finalists were contacted for an interview with the governor's chief legal counsel. Graydon was one of the final two.

We were so excited about the impending appointment! We even took comfort in the fact that God had allowed Graydon eleven more years of practicing law to prepare him for the position. He would honor God in that position, and after working so hard to secure the appointment, we were expectant that Graydon's hour had come.

The other finalist received the appointment.

I wept bitter tears after that crushing defeat. "God, I don't understand what you are doing!" I cried. "To come so close twice, only to fail, is so painful I can't stand it! What is it you want us to learn? Humility? Patience? Disappointment? To be content with what we have? Then why in the world were we so sure we were doing what you wanted us to do?"

I struggled with disillusionment. Here I was, a Christian motivational speaker, and I was doubting whether God really cared about the affairs of our lives or about our heartache. I would get weepy in church, in my car, or in the grocery store, and I hated it. "You'd better toughen me up, Lord, because I'm a mess!"

I finally came to the conclusion that it was fruitless to ask *why*. It was far more productive to sincerely ask, "Lord, what would you have us do now?"

I sometimes wondered if the pain would go away, but found peace in taking my focus off myself and putting it back on my Savior.

Three years passed and both Graydon's practice and my speaking ministry were thriving. Then one day Graydon phoned me to say that the longtime Newyago County probate court judge was retiring before his term of office ended. Once again, the governor would appoint a successor. I held the phone in silence for a moment, the experiences of the past flooding back.

"What do you think, honey?" he asked. "I'm not even going to call for the application papers unless you are at peace about this. I know how hard this was on you the last time, and we don't have to go through it all again."

"But, Graydon, this job is your dream. You would work with troubled families and the elderly. You would *love* it."

"Well, the competition will be stiff, and the *really* bad news is that whoever gets the appointment will only serve till the end of the year and then will have to stand for re-election."

My mind reeled with the impact of his statement. On the heels of the complicated and stressful appointment process would be the overwhelming task of going through an election? Should Graydon risk leaving his busy law practice for such a gamble?

Yes. After prayerfully considering every aspect and again seeking wise counsel, Graydon applied. This time we "knew the ropes" well enough that some of the stress was eliminated from the process. Graydon received powerful, unexpected endorsements from influential leaders. Voters deluged the governor's office with letters of recommendation. Once again two finalists were contacted. Again, Graydon was one of the two.

For most of the process, I was at peace. However, just a week before the final interview, I had a panic attack. I had never experienced such a thing before, but I just lost it. I remember opening my Bible at the kitchen table in a state of agitation and not making sense of anything. I got up, walked into the family room, and started crying. I reached up, I suppose to try to grab onto God, and cried aloud, "I'm afraid! We've come this far before only to lose, and I'm so afraid of failing again. Please help me!" I crumpled to my knees by the couch and wept.

When my sobs subsided, a quietness settled over me. I got up, walked back into the kitchen, and sat back down at the table, turning my attention to the passage of Scripture I had walked away from earlier. It was Psalm 107:28–31.

> Then they cried out to the LORD in their trouble,
>   and he brought them out of their distress.
> He stilled the storm to a whisper;
>   the waves of the sea were hushed.
> They were glad when it grew calm,
>   and he guided them to their desired haven.
> Let them give thanks to the LORD for his unfailing love
>   and his wonderful deeds for men.

I remember sitting at the table and feeling a sense of completeness wash over me. I recognized that God not only heard the cry of my heart, but that he also was totally in control of our situation and always had been. I placed a trembling hand over the sacred words and started to praise him.

Later that morning I ran errands, stopping by the pharmacy to pick up a prescription. It wasn't ready, so I wandered through the store, stopping at a sale table to look at some small inspirational posters. At first I thought they were all the same humorous design, but on the bottom of the stack I pulled out one that left me momentarily frozen to the spot. It was a picture of five men pressed against the wind, rowing a boat on rough water, with thunderous clouds threatening overhead. An abbreviated verse was imprinted on the poster, which read, "They cried out to the Lord in their trouble and he brought them out of their distress. He stilled the storm to a whisper; the waves of the sea were hushed. They were glad when it grew calm, and he guided them to their desired haven."

Beneath the verse it said, "The rewards of the journey far outweigh the risk of leaving the harbor."

From that point, my confidence never wavered. Graydon went through the final interview and called home afterward. He was quietly confident that the governor's call would come. It did. Graydon sold his law practice of twenty-two years and joyfully took office in April. Then our worst fear was realized when he was challenged for the judgeship in the following November election. God gave us an amazing peace, and we never doubted that he was directing our path. The campaign was exhausting, but this time Graydon won by almost 70 percent of the vote.

A Passionate Prayer

Dear Heavenly Father, it seems easy to run to you when I'm in trouble, but I'll admit right now that I have no affection for the waiting room. Please help me to keep on trusting you when things don't go like I think they should. You've been so faithful in the past. Help me to concentrate on the mighty things you've done before, both in my life and in my heart and in the lives of others. Please provide the patience and peace of mind I'll need while I "wait" for your direction, and use my attitude and the circumstances of my life to bring honor and glory to you.

In the precious name of Jesus, Amen.

The Scripture Reading: John 11:1–45

Now a man named Lazarus was sick. He was from Bethany, the village of Mary and her sister Martha. This Mary, whose brother Lazarus now lay sick, was the same one who poured perfume on the Lord and wiped his feet with her hair. So the sisters sent word to Jesus, "Lord, the one you love is sick."

When he heard this, Jesus said, "This sickness will not end in death. No, it is for God's glory so that God's Son may be glorified through it." Jesus loved Martha and her sister and Lazarus. Yet when he heard that Lazarus was sick, he stayed where he was two more days.

Then he said to his disciples, "Let us go back to Judea."

"But Rabbi," they said, "a short while ago the Jews tried to stone you, and yet you are going back there?"

Jesus answered, "Are there not twelve hours of daylight? A man who walks by day will not stumble, for he sees by this world's light. It is when he walks by night that he stumbles, for he has no light."

After he had said this, he went on to tell them, "Our friend Lazarus has fallen asleep; but I am going there to wake him up."

His disciples replied, "Lord, if he sleeps, he will get better." Jesus had been speaking of his death, but his disciples thought he meant natural sleep.

So then he told them plainly, "Lazarus is dead, and for your sake I am glad I was not there, so that you may believe. But let us go to him."

Then Thomas (called Didymus) said to the rest of the disciples, "Let us also go, that we may die with him."

On his arrival, Jesus found that Lazarus had already been in the tomb for four days. Bethany was less than two miles from Jerusalem, and many Jews had come to Martha and Mary to comfort them in the loss of their brother. When Martha heard that Jesus was coming, she went out to meet him, but Mary stayed at home.

"Lord," Martha said to Jesus, "if you had been here, my brother would not have died. But I know that even now God will give you whatever you ask."

Jesus said to her, "Your brother will rise again."

Martha answered, "I know he will rise again in the resurrection at the last day."

Jesus said to her, "I am the resurrection and the life. He who believes in me will live, even though he dies; and whoever lives and believes in me will never die. Do you believe this?"

"Yes, Lord," she told him, "I believe that you are the Christ, the Son of God, who was to come into the world."

And after she had said this, she went back and called her sister Mary aside. "The Teacher is here," she said, "and is asking for you." When Mary heard this, she got up quickly and went to him. Now Jesus had not yet entered the village, but was still at the place where Martha had met him. When the Jews who had been with Mary in the house, comforting her, noticed how quickly she got up and went out, they followed her, supposing she was going to the tomb to mourn there.

When Mary reached the place where Jesus was and saw him, she fell at his feet and said, "Lord, if you had been here, my brother would not have died."

When Jesus saw her weeping, and the Jews who had come along with her also weeping, he was deeply moved in spirit and troubled. "Where have you laid him?" he asked.

"Come and see, Lord," they replied.

Jesus wept.

Then the Jews said, "See how he loved him!"

But some of them said, "Could not he who opened the eyes of the blind man have kept this man from dying?"

Jesus, once more deeply moved, came to the tomb. It was a cave with a stone laid across the entrance. "Take away the stone," he said.

"But, Lord," said Martha, the sister of the dead man, "by this time there is a bad odor, for he has been there four days."

Then Jesus said, "Did I not tell you that if you believed, you would see the glory of God?"

So they took away the stone. Then Jesus looked up and said, "Father, I thank you that you have heard me. I knew that you always hear me, but I said this for the benefit of the people standing here, that they may believe that you sent me."

When he had said this, Jesus called in a loud voice, "Lazarus, come out!" The dead man came out, his hands and feet wrapped with strips of linen, and a cloth around his face.

Jesus said to them, "Take off the grave clothes and let him go."

Therefore many of the Jews who had come to visit Mary, and had seen what Jesus did, put their faith in him.

Final Note: This story was recorded by John, the brother of James. First as a disciple and then as an apostle, he personally observed the ministry of Jesus Christ. This account was probably written between AD 85 and 90, after Jerusalem was destroyed in AD 70 and before John was exiled to the island of Patmos in his old age. He authored the Gospel of John, three New Testament letters, and the book of Revelation.

10

Escape from Death Row!
A Story about Deliverance and Answered Prayer

We stared at the screen, holding our breath as the villain in the story used his power against the peasants in the village for his own evil gain!

My neighbor Bernadine and I were watching a recent video presentation of the story of Robin Hood, and the character of the Sheriff of Nottingham was evil indeed. He taxed the people mercilessly and burned their village. He accused honest men of blasphemy against God and put them to death so he could confiscate their property. He put men and boys to death for poaching game to feed their families, used women selfishly, manipulated religious leaders for his own purposes, sought the advice of a witch, and imprisoned Maid Marian! It was a great relief when Robin Hood came to the rescue!

I later dug out my encyclopedia and found that although ballads and stories about Robin Hood abound from the thirteenth and fourteenth centuries, little evidence actually exists to support the legend. Still, I was rather haunted by the character of that sheriff. Then it dawned on me that he reminded me of an actual character from history who behaved in much the same way.

His name was Herod Agrippa I, and he was a bad one. He came into power as the appointed king of the Jewish nation several years after the death and resurrection of Jesus Christ. I want to fill you in briefly on the events that led up to this story before I introduce you to Herod any further.

When his hour had come, Jesus had been crucified and buried in a tomb. After three days, he rose from the dead, and some time later, after meeting with his disciples, he rose up into heaven in front of many witnesses, promising to come again one day to receive all believers unto himself. In the meantime, his Holy Spirit would be with them to teach and to guide, and the believers were to go and spread the gospel of Christ to every nation. This they did. The gospel of Jesus Christ had incredible power to break down social and cultural barriers, creating a new people of God.

This rapidly growing movement was a great threat to the Jewish religious leaders, and its Christian followers became the objects of harassment and cruel persecution. In spite of this, the church continued to grow, spreading throughout the Roman Empire and beyond.

Peter's Story

Herod Agrippa surveyed the vast arena, congratulating himself once again for his foresight in building a facility that could serve so many purposes. As the appointed king of the Jewish nation under the control of the Roman Empire, he used the coliseum for games and competitions that delighted the Romans and Greeks. Now he had found a use for it that pleased the Jews very much as well.

They weren't easy to please, that was for sure. They had reluctantly accepted him, since his own grandmother had been Jewish, but he was careful to observe all the religious holidays to keep them pacified. Then with the advent of the fast-growing Christian movement, he had found an opportunity to gain unprecedented favor with the religious leaders: he arrested some members of the Christian church, his intention being to persecute them. This so pleased the Jews that he had boldly gone after the leaders of the movement.

The apostle James had most recently been executed here with the sword, and Herod had discovered that beheadings were spectacles that drew large crowds. Some had cheered and some had wept, he recalled with an evil smile, and the Jewish leaders had been adoring of him since then. The execution had been such a popular event that he had decided to take further action and had the apostle Peter arrested.

Herod walked over to the judgment seat, where he would sit when the "defendant" was brought out, and he stroked his hand over the rich upholstery. Then he cast his gaze once more over the vast arena, imagining the cheering crowd. The religious holiday would end tomorrow, and while the city was still crowded with Jews who had come from outside the area for the festival, he intended to entertain his subjects once again.

His prey was in the inner prison at that very moment, and Herod had taken care that the slippery fisherman would be well guarded. He had heard that the man had mysteriously escaped from prison once before, and he had no intention of disappointing his eager audience. With a self-satisfied sigh, he snapped his fingers for his attendants to escort him back to his quarters, where a fine dinner awaited him.

Peter murmured an apology to the guard on his left as he shifted his weight, dragging the chain attached to the shackle on his left wrist across his hip so he could turn to lie on his right side. A single lantern was fastened to the wall across the room, casting eerie shadows on Peter and his two companions. There was an earthenware pot for sewage in the corner, and the straw on the floor completed the amenities his host had provided.

As an important political prisoner, Peter had no less than sixteen soldiers assigned to guard him. Working in shifts, four of them at a time had the responsibility of keeping him under lock and key until the public trial, which was scheduled for the next day. With his wrists shackled, Peter was in close company, since two of the soldiers were chained right to him. Two more stood guard outside the door.

What a miserable job these fellows have, he thought. *They might as well be prisoners themselves.* With a sigh, he turned his thoughts to the gravity of his own situation.

The realization that his death would very likely follow his trial brought a strange mix of emotions. There was so much work yet to do in encouraging and building up the rapidly growing Christian church. A pang of regret struck him as he contemplated missing being a part of the unfolding miracle of the fast-growing movement. Leadership was so important. God would simply have to raise up someone else in his place.

That thought stirred the memory of the recent death of James. How his execution had grieved the Christian brothers and sisters! He thought of the gathering of believers that had met at the home of Mark's mother, Mary, after they heard the news, and he squeezed his eyes shut at the memory of their anguish. They were such a precious band of believers. He had no doubt that they knew of his arrest and of Herod's plans for tomorrow. They would be praying for God to work a miracle that would somehow save his life. It was a comfort to think of them praying. If God did not choose to intervene, well, then he would see Jesus tomorrow, and that thought also brought him comfort. How wonderful it would be to see his precious Lord again!

His thoughts wandered further. He would see Stephen, dear Stephen, who had been stoned to death. And he would see James, his old fishing buddy; they would be together again. They had sailed the Sea of Galilee together many times, wrapping their hands around the rough ropes and casting their nets with John and Andrew and their fathers. Then Jesus had come along and changed all their lives. He had taught them to be fishers of men.

With his cloak balled up under his head for a pillow, Peter inhaled deeply and closed his eyes. The peace of God washed over him, and in spite of his dire circumstances, he slept.

In the late hours of the night, Peter was startled awake. Something had struck him on the side, and he heard a voice order in a loud whisper, "Quick, get up!"

Rising to one elbow, he squinted his eyes, trying to adjust to the brilliant light that filled the cell. The sight before him shocked him into wakefulness. Standing in the cell was an angel of the Lord! Jerking his attention to the guards, he saw that they were just as they had been when he had fallen asleep and totally unaware of the brilliant light and the angel. As Peter pushed himself to his feet, the shackles on his wrists fell away.

"Put on your clothes and sandals," the angel instructed.

Peter reached for his leather girdle and tied it over his tunic. He bent to adjust his sandals, thinking, *I must be dreaming.*

"Now wrap your cloak around you and follow me," said the angel.

With one parting look at the unmoving guards, Peter followed his guide out the door, casting furtive glances around the passageway as they passed the first and second guard posts. The soldiers were standing at attention but didn't seem to see a thing! What a strange dream this was.

Finally reaching the outer gate that led to the city, Peter was astounded to see the heavy iron gate creak open all by itself! They went through it, and the angel led him down the length of one street and then disappeared.

Peter stood there for a moment in confusion. The chill of the night air penetrated his consciousness, and he reached up to touch his face with his hands. With shocking clarity, he realized that what had just happened had not been a dream at all! He said aloud, "Without a doubt, I know the Lord sent his angel and rescued me from Herod's clutches and from everything the Jewish people were planning."

With that realization came the awareness that he was a fugitive from Herod's prison and that an alarm could be sounded at any moment! Feeling certain that he needed to tell at least some of the believers what God had done, he hurried through the dark streets to the home of Mary, the mother of Mark. To his great joy, he could see that there were dim lamps still burning, even at this early-morning hour. After checking for pursuers from both directions of the street, he knocked at the outer entrance to the large home.

The believers had crowded into Mary's home at the news of Peter's arrest and pending trial for an all-night prayer vigil. The recent violent death of the apostle James was a raw reminder of how dire Peter's situation was, and they had come together to petition the Lord on his behalf. As the hours went by and the dawn approached, they poured out their hearts to God, asking for a miracle. Would God strike down their enemies? Could the trial be halted by a powerful defense? Hour after hour they prayed, but the likelihood of Peter becoming the next martyr made their hearts heavy.

But the earnest murmurings and heart-cries of the Christians were heard by the One they petitioned.

What was that sound? Rhoda, a young servant girl, looked up from her place of prayer to listen. There it was again! It sounded like someone knocking at the outer gate. She rose quietly, not wanting to disturb those deeply in prayer around her, and slipped out the door and into the courtyard. Sure enough, someone was knocking on the gate, quite insistently. Her heart thudded in her chest at the thought of recent arrests of Christians in the area, and she hesitated in opening the door.

"Let me in! Hurry! Open the gate. It's me, Peter! Please let me in!"

Recognizing the voice of Peter, Rhoda was so shocked that, after standing stock-still for a moment, she dashed back inside to tell the others. In her excitement, she neglected to pull back the bolt and left Peter standing outside in the darkened street.

Bursting into the house, she called out, "Peter is here! I heard his voice! Peter is here!"

Deeply engrossed in fervent prayer, the group chastised Rhoda for the rude interruption. Committed to praying the night through, they motioned her away.

"But I tell you, he was at the gate!"

"Did you see him?" asked Mary, the owner of the home.

"No, but I heard his voice!" Rhoda answered.

"Then it must have been his angel," someone offered. Then, startled by the thought, the person asked, "Could they have executed him already?"

Mary stood and headed for the courtyard. "I think I had better see what this is about."

"I heard his voice," Rhoda insisted. "Oh, dear! I never opened the gate!" The girl turned around and ran after her mistress. The others followed as well, crowding into the courtyard.

Peter continued knocking, almost despairing that anyone would come back to let him in. Were they afraid to open the door for fear of arrest? *I can hardly blame them*, he thought, knocking a bit louder and casting a worried glance down the street in the direction from which he had come. The authorities might be upon him at any moment. It had been easier to get out of prison than to get into this house!

Finally, he heard people approaching, and he called out in a loud whisper. "Open the gate! It's me, Peter! Hurry!"

Mary rushed to pull back the bolt and joyfully welcomed her friend. Astonished, the Christians all started talking at once, but Peter motioned with his hand for silence and urged them back into the house.

"Don't raise the lamplight," he cautioned. "I only have a few minutes before I must flee, but I need to tell you what the Lord has done this night. We don't want to call attention to ourselves in the neighborhood or it will raise the suspicion of the authorities!"

When they were quiet, Peter related the astounding events of the hour that had just passed and declared the wonderful deliverance the Lord had granted him. "Thank you, my dear friends, for your faithful prayers! God answered your petitions in a way we would never have imagined! I must go now, for your safety as well as my own, but be sure to tell James, the brother of Jesus, what has happened, and pass on this news to our other brothers and sisters in Christ, so they will be encouraged in the Lord as well."

Then, embracing his friends, Peter turned to go, pausing only to take the small bag of provisions Mary pressed upon him. He slipped away into the darkness and departed for another place.

The following morning the prison was in an uproar. When soldiers arrived for the morning changing of the guard, those that were stationed to watch Peter through the night discovered to their horror that their prisoner was gone. A frantic search was made throughout the prison; after all, if Peter had somehow managed to escape his cell, he certainly could not have made it through the iron gates at the entrance. But their desperate search offered no clue to Peter's disappearance, and with dread, they sent word to Herod.

Herod arose and dressed in his royal robes, eager for the events that would take place that day. Humming tunelessly, he chose the jewelry he would wear for his important public appearance and, slipping on several rings, motioned for his servant to place a heavy gold chain around his neck.

A knock at the door was followed by Blastus, his trusted servant, who announced that the captain of the guard was there to see him.

"Send him in!" Herod said jovially. "I would like to hear how my prize is pleading for my mercy this morning! If he begs in the arena, it will make for a far more entertaining demonstration than if he stands there like a dumb lamb going to the slaughter!"

The soldier stepped into the room, bowed to the king, and then stood in awkward silence for a moment.

"Well, speak!" Herod ordered. "Do you bear news or not?"

"Sir, the prisoner has escaped."

Herod's head jerked up, and he stared in disbelief at the soldier standing before him. "What?" he roared. "Surely you do not dare to jest with me!"

"The apostle Peter is gone. The guards saw nothing, heard nothing. We have made a complete search of the prison and cannot find him."

"You *will* find him, do you hear me?" Herod shouted. "If he is not found, there will be a high price to pay!"

When a thorough search was completed, all to no avail, Herod, in his fury, had a public demonstration after all. All sixteen soldiers who had been assigned to guard Peter were put to death.

Later, Herod left Jerusalem to travel to his home in Caesarea, where he stayed for a while. While he was there, the leaders from the coastal cities of Tyre and Sidon gained the confidence of Blastus, Herod's servant. They desired an audience with the king, because he held the strings to their food supply, and they arranged for a meeting through his servant.

On the day of the meeting, Herod, dressed in his royal robes, sat on his throne and delivered a formal public address to the people. Playing to his ego, the people shouted, "This is the voice of a god, not of a man."

Herod basked for just a moment in the glory that should have been God's alone. Then the angel of the Lord struck him down. He was eaten by worms and died.

But the word of God continued to spread.

Digging Deeper

Who's who? Before we get into the major aspects of the story, it would be helpful to clarify the identity of two of the people in the story.

Another Mary? The Mary in this story was not Mary, the mother of Jesus, and she was not Mary, the sister of Martha and Lazarus. This woman was Mary, the mother of John Mark the evangelist, who as a young man was a traveling companion to three great early missionaries: Paul, Barnabas, and Peter. He was also one of the first to record the events of Jesus's life in his book, the Gospel of Mark. His mother, Mary, was a wealthy widow who dedicated her large house in Jerusalem to the Lord's work. "During the days of terrible persecution the saints in Jerusalem gathered regularly in her lovely home not only for the reading and exposition of the Word, but also to pray for afflicted saints."[1] Evidently Peter had been there often, because Rhoda, the servant girl, recognized his voice.

Mary was a very common name and was derived from the name Miriam. (Remember the Old Testament woman by that name whose life was the subject of chapter 3 in this book?)

Another James? The apostle James was put to death by Herod Agrippa before Peter was arrested. When Peter was ready to leave the prayer group at Mary's house, he instructed the group in verse 17 to tell James and some others all that had happened. This James was one of Jesus's own brothers; that is, he was the son of Mary, Jesus's mother, and her husband, Joseph. He became one of the key Christian leaders in Jerusalem during this dangerous time for the early church.

Now let's dig deeper into this powerful story and take a closer look at several challenges that faced Peter and the early Christians and also a look at the key resource they used to deal with those challenges.

Herod Agrippa I was a powerful and evil enemy. He was an evil ruler who came from a long line of evil leaders. His grandfather, Herod the Great, was the ruler who, when he learned from the wise men that Jesus was born, tried to kill him by ordering that all the baby boys in Bethlehem be murdered. His sister, Herodias, was responsible for John the Baptist being put to death (Mark 6:17–28). Herod Agrippa I followed in their wicked footsteps.

The Romans had appointed him to rule over most of Palestine, including the territories of Galilee, Perea, Judea, and

Samaria. He persecuted the Christians in order to please the Jewish leaders who opposed them, hoping that would solidify his position. Peter was arrested during the Feast of Unleavened Bread, the week-long festival directly following Passover. This was a strategic move, since more Jews were in the city than usual and Herod could impress the most people.[2]

Robertson's *Word Pictures in the New Testament* gives a little more detail about Herod: "He was a favourite of Caligula the Roman Emperor and was anxious to placate his Jewish subjects while retaining the favour of the Romans. So he built theatres and held games for the Romans and Greeks and slew the Christians to please the Jews."[3]

Peter was trapped in bondage. The enemy had Peter in total physical bondage. Determined that nothing would spoil his evil agenda, Herod assigned sixteen soldiers to guard Peter until his trial. Robertson gives extra insight into Peter's captivity: "[There were] four soldiers in each quaternion, two on the inside with the prisoner (chained to him) and two on the outside, in shifts of six hours each, sixteen soldiers in all, the usual Roman custom."[4]

Herod had covered every base and tied every knot necessary to insure that Peter would remain in his clutches and be available for his evil purposes. Matthew Henry noted: "Peter was kept in prison with a great deal of care, so that it was altogether impossible, either by force or by stealth, to get him out; but prayer was made without ceasing of the church unto God for him."[5]

Peter had a solace and secret weapon. A major emphasis of the early church was the importance of prayer.

"The first prayer meeting of the new movement was notable for its inclusiveness, particularly of women (Acts 1:14). Jewish religious gatherings separated men and women and assigned them different roles. By contrast, the apostles were joined by women who had followed Christ, including his mother. Together they formed a unified group of dedicated followers. God intended all of them to be his witnesses."[6]

The story of Peter's dramatic escape from prison is coupled with the information that "the church was earnestly praying to God for him" (Acts 12:5). The King James Version says that "prayer was made without ceasing by the Church unto God for him." After his deliverance, Peter made a stop at one location, the home of a widow named Mary, where an all-night prayer meeting was being held on his behalf. The Christians were using prayer, their most powerful weapon, in waging spiritual warfare against their enemy.

"Herod's plan was undoubtedly to execute Peter, but the believers were praying for Peter's safety. The earnest prayer of the church significantly affected the outcome of these events."[7]

The enemy was indeed powerful, and the situation, humanly speaking, hopeless. But God intervened. The battle was won through prayer.

Peter experienced supernatural deliverance. Sleeping while bound in chains, he was first nudged awake by none other than an angel of the Lord, and then several highly unusual occurrences followed. A brilliant light filled the dark cell. Peter's chains fell off. The guards, all of them, were oblivious to his movements. The heavy iron door opened automatically. What was happening seemed so impossible that Peter thought he was dreaming or seeing a vision! Then the angel led him down a street and disappeared. When he pinched himself and realized he was actually on a street outside of the prison, he declared out loud that God had delivered him from Herod's clutches and from the plans of the Jews.

God had worked a remarkable miracle in Peter's life, but now it was up to him to take personal action.

How can this story apply to your life?

Are there parallels between this story and our lives? There sure are.

Herod was a powerful and evil enemy. He, with his chilling tactics, was easy to recognize as a major enemy of the early Christians, but the evil one who controlled him is actually our enemy too.

People don't talk much about Satan these days, but he's alive and well, targeting Christians every day for defeat. He would love to see homes broken, lives lost to suicide or violence, addictions, bitterness, and despair—anything that keeps Christians from living joyful and victorious lives. Sherrer and Garlock, in their book, *A Woman's Guide to Spiritual Warfare*, list both his methods and his character from Scripture. Satan is:

crafty (Genesis 3:1)

the deceiver (Genesis 3:13)

the foe and the avenger (Psalm 8:2)

the destroyer (Isaiah 54:16)

the tempter (Matthew 4:3; 1 Thessalonians 3:5)

ruler of demons [Beelzebub] (Matthew 12:24)

a murderer (John 8:44)

a liar and the father of lies (John 8:44)

the evil one (Matthew 6:13; John 17:15)

the god of this age (2 Corinthians 4:4)

a masquerader, pretending to be an angel of light (2 Corinthians 11:14)

the ruler of the kingdom of the air (Ephesians 2:2)

the dragon, . . . that ancient serpent (Revelation 12:7–9)

the accuser (Revelation 12:10)[8]

Yikes! That list makes me want to run the other way! However, I'm afraid that far too often we don't recognize Satan for who and what he is, and we flirt with the temptation he offers rather than going to war against him.

From a prison cell, Paul wrote to the Ephesian Christians and said: "Finally, be strong in the Lord and in his mighty power. Put on the full armor of God so that you can take your stand against the devil's schemes" (Ephesians 6:10–11). We need to heed that same advice and realize that we have some awesome resources to protect and free us from the enemy's hold on our lives.

Peter was trapped in bondage. Peter's bondage was tangible in that he was bound with shackles he could see and feel. Many women today are also in bondage. Most are not bound physically, but rather emotionally and spiritually. Very often Christian women hide their bondage behind a cheerful smile, the facade of a happy marriage and family, charitable activity in their church or community, or behind other various masks, all while the enemy smiles smugly.

As a retreat and conference speaker, I have been approached by many women who are in bondage. Some are controlled by fear, anger, or memories of an abusive past. Many women struggle with guilt over secret addictions. They play computer games, watch soap operas, or read one romance novel after another to the point that they neglect their families, jobs, or other important responsibilities. Some have over-the-counter drug addictions or are addicted to alcohol. A growing number of women are addicted to pornography or chat rooms on the Internet. Others are defeated by anger, shame, worry, or despair over the behavior of their children or their spouses. They have divided homes that often seem like inescapable war zones.

At a large women's retreat in Canada, a young woman asked if we could speak privately. We found a quiet spot in the hotel lobby, and she told me how much she loved sharing in the music ministry at her church. Then she handed me a picture of her beautiful family. "I love them very much," she said, "but I've been having an affair with another man for almost two years. I meet him on business trips, and my husband has no idea. I told myself that I would have fun for a little while and then I'd walk away, but I just can't give him up." She was in bondage.

Sharon was a young mom with a shopping addiction. If she needed a "lift" emotionally, she would head for the mall and buy things. Her husband didn't notice at first, but finally he complained about her spending. Rather than curb her habit, she spent more and then borrowed hundreds of dollars from a friend to pay the bills before her husband found out, trapping herself in more guilt and debt. Bondage.

Bondage is a controlling factor in the lives of many women. Shame often keeps them from seeking help. The awesome news is that Jesus loves us, and he came to set captives free. I know this is true, because Jesus set me free, and I have seen him change the lives of many others.

Peter had a solace and secret weapon. The Christians in the early church took prayer seriously. They knew that apart from God's intervention in their lives and circumstances, things were pretty hopeless. They risked meeting together, and they collectively poured out their hearts to God. J. Vernon McGee said, "They didn't come before God with a kind of grocery-list prayer. They went before God and earnestly prayed that this man Simon Peter be delivered. Their hearts were in their prayers."[9]

The results of those prayers were freedom from fear and peace of mind for Peter, to the extent that he was able to sleep soundly the night before his trial. Another result was a supernatural deliverance that was better by far than what they had hoped for! Plus, God used the experience to strengthen their faith and their resolve to spread the gospel. In addition to all that, God literally wiped out their enemy, Herod.

Do you take prayer seriously? Is it a vital part of your life? Do you put your heart into your prayers? Do you make the effort to pray collectively with others who will share your burdens? Do you pray specifically for your family members? Many times Christians are blinded to the fact that living a victorious Christian life requires practicing spiritual warfare, in which prayer is a powerful weapon.

Peter experienced supernatural deliverance. God's hand in Peter's deliverance is irrefutable. Isn't it interesting that when God sent his answer to Peter in the form of an angel, Peter figured it was just too good to be true—it must be a dream? And when God brought an answer to prayer to their very door, the Christians were so busy praying that they didn't immediately recognize that God had answered? I find some humor in that, but comfort too in the realization that although their faith wasn't as strong as it could have been, God heard their cry and sent his answer.

I close this last chapter of *Passionate Faith* by sharing my friend Katie's touching, life-changing, faith story. I do this for two reasons. First, because it will encourage many women who have struggled to find wholeness, and second, because it emphasizes the key elements of Peter's story: a powerful enemy, bondage to fear and addiction, the power of prayer, and freedom in Christ. It is also particularly fitting to end the book with her story, because Katie came to Christ after reading the Bible for herself.

Katie suffered from shyness and had low self-esteem to the point that she hated going out in public. She forced herself to do the family grocery shopping but chose markets that were open late at night so she would encounter as few people as possible. A gifted and highly intelligent young woman, she longed for friendship and purpose in her life but felt trapped and hopeless in her circumstances. She was in bondage, both to her fear and to an addiction to an old habit.

We met the day our children enrolled in nursery school. It was apparent that Katie was painfully shy, so our first conversation was a bit awkward, but I learned that she was the wife of a corporate executive, a devoted young mom, and an artist. When she learned that I needed some art work done for my business, she surprised us both by showing up on my doorstep a week later with some creative work under her arm. We then agreed that she would create the corporate logo for my company.

A week or so later, Katie again showed up unexpectedly. I invited her in and sat down with her at the dining room table. I had company coming that night and plenty to do, but I felt an unmistakable urging to share with Katie on a deeper level than I had on her other brief visits.

"Katie, I am so very glad that we met the day we brought our kids to nursery school!"

She grinned back at me and nodded. "Me too."

"Well," I continued, "if we're going to get to know each other even better, there's something I'd like to tell you about myself." Smiling at her across the table, I plunged in. "I'm a Christian, and I'd like to explain to you what that means to me."

I went on to tell Katie that I had grown up in a wonderful Christian home but realized at a young age that I needed a personal relationship with God. I told her how I had invited him into my life and the difference it had made as I allowed him to direct me. I even shared how my husband had searched for meaning in his life and found the truth in God's Word, the Bible. When I was finished, Katie gave me a blunt response.

"I suppose that was an interesting story, Jennie, but now I want to tell you something about myself. I'm *not* interested! When I was a teenager, I boxed up everything in my life that resembled religion and labeled it 'childishness.' I certainly hope that every time we're together, you're not going to get religious!"

I felt like I had been slapped, but I managed a small, apologetic smile. "I never meant to offend you, Katie, and I'll make you a promise right now. I will never talk to you about religion or spiritual things unless you bring it up first. But I'm going to make a second promise. I promise to pray for you every day, that somehow, without me saying a word, you will see Christ in me and want to know him, too."

She left abruptly, but after about a week she came back. Our visits were a little awkward at first, but they soon smoothed out. And every day I prayed for my friend.

Several months passed, and one morning the phone rang. "Jennie, look out your kitchen window and tell me what you see," Katie said.

It had snowed the night before, and the sight outside was breathtaking. "I see an inch of snow on every twig and branch on the trees," I began. "The sun is shining, and the snow seems to be sparkling in its brilliance. It's beautiful, Katie."

"Yeah, here too. Jennie, remember that day I stopped by your house and you told me that big long story about God, and how you had invited his Son, Jesus, to come into your life, and how God changed your husband's life, and all that?"

I smiled into the telephone receiver. "I certainly do, Katie, and I hope you realize that I've kept my promise not to bring this subject up! I've kept the other promise, too, though. I've prayed for you every day."

"I figured you were praying," she said quietly, and then continued. "I was so angry that day I could have physically struck you, Jennie. Did you realize that? Then when I got home and several days went by, I found myself at a terrible loss. I discovered that my artistic sight had left me. I used to be able to look out my window at a scene like you just described and re-create it on paper. Suddenly that gift was missing, and it frightened and angered me. I blamed you. I fell back into my old habit of getting high every day, hoping it would mellow me out and get my creativity flowing again, but my frustration only increased."

As I listened to Katie's words, my heart was pounding furiously, and I found myself praying for wisdom. She went on.

"Then I decided I'd take the challenge your husband took and read the Bible for myself. I'd even start in the book of John like you suggested, and when I finished it, I'd confront you with the fact that it was worthless. But that's not quite what happened.

"I was reading a chapter a day, feeling pretty smug that it meant nothing, when I got to the ninth chapter of John where it says that Jesus didn't just come to give sight to the blind, but to show those who *think* they see that they're really blind themselves. Well, I read that and was overwhelmed with grief at my own spiritual blindness. I got down on my knees, can you believe that? And I cried out to God and told him I desperately needed him to help me see, and that I'd made such a mess of my life."

I felt tears slipping down my cheeks as I listened. "Oh, Katie. Do you realize what you are saying? You've opened up your heart to God!"

"Yes, I did, Jennie, and this incredible peace and joy came over me. I didn't call you right away, in case the feeling went away, but it hasn't. It's just grown. I finished the book of John and started reading the whole New Testament. Do you think I could come to your house and go through the books in your library? There's so much more I want to learn."

Katie's new life was awesome to watch unfold. The once-reclusive young woman found wholeness in Jesus Christ. Over the next three years, she wrote me eleven beautiful letters that chronicled her spiritual awakening and growth. I'd like to simply quote from the letters, so that you will understand the miracle God worked in her life.

1) It surprises me how much faith and trust are such a daily element in my new life. It's far more than just taking an original, daring, trusting step when you turn to God.

2) God is starting to reach down into my life (I like to think of it as my "soul's house") and is doing some "housecleaning." He is carefully and lovingly examining some very old issues in my life. This problem is like a big old moldy piece of overstuffed furniture hiding in the basement of my "soul's house," and it's time to get rid of it.

3) I have felt a great desire to relate to you all that has happened since I last saw you. The most thrilling part of all is the spiritual growth I am experiencing as I read the Bible, and also as I pray.

4) My prayers have grown to the point where my mind begins to fill with praises and thank yous, with repentance, requests for myself and for others, and it goes on and on. Prayer has become a vibrant, living experience!

5) In my old life, I could either pigeonhole a problem, bury it, deny it existed, smoke myself into another world, or take a drink to numb the pain. Now all those old ways of dealing with things are no more, and I think God is allowing these things to surface to be finally dealt with—to make my life real and in order again.

6) I am involved in two Friendship Bible Coffees. They are high spots in the week for me and I feel that the women I have met are the start to some very good friendships.

7) *The truth God continues to reveal to me fills me with an inexpressible awe, happiness, and gratitude.*

8) *I have begun to see how God loves and cares for all parts of my life, and that it is his intention for me to achieve wholeness in every area, through him. He offers his hand through all of it. I don't need to struggle alone. I am being transformed piece by piece, as more and more of his light seeps in. He reveals himself to me in digestible stages.*

9) *I see the reality of the transformation and real healing that is possible through God. The process of becoming whole is beyond words! As I offer up to him everything I am able to, he gives me back more than I thought possible. . . . He really can make us into new people; and as I look around me and see even the hardest of hearts and distorted personalities, I can have hope in him who can truly do anything. That is easy for me to believe now that he has changed my own life so dramatically.*

10) *Looking back, I see that I've come through some dangerous territory. I was tempted to go after a facsimile of what I really wanted. . . . That's the real test, isn't it? Being able to turn down what you think you want the most because you know it isn't right. I had to struggle and tussle with it for two months. The only real peace I had in that time was when I would say, "Okay, God, it's yours."*

11) *I've come through all this, clinging to that one state of being—of being right in his eyes through Christ, and preserving that rightness by offering my total self up to him. Thank you for reading all this, Jennie. I am warmed to know that we can always talk to each other no matter how long the passage of time, because the heart of which we speak is timeless.*

Love, Katie

A Passionate Prayer

Dear Heavenly Father, thank you for listening when I pray. The fact that you care about the details of my life and intervene, protect, and lead me fills me with confidence as I live through uncertain days. Thank you for your amazing power to free me and others I am burdened for from the shackles of sin. You are truly an awesome God!

Thank you for the Bible, your precious, holy Word, that teaches me how to live by faith and encourages me to pray. Lord, I give you permission to reach into my life and houseclean my soul's house. Please help me to hunger after righteousness and to reject those things that would tempt me away from a right relationship with you.

I love you, dear Father. Thank you for loving me.

In the powerful name of Jesus, Amen.

The Scripture Reading: Acts 12:1–24

It was about this time that King Herod arrested some who belonged to the church, intending to persecute them. He had James, the brother of John, put to death with the sword. When he saw that this pleased the Jews, he proceeded to seize Peter also. This happened during the Feast of Unleavened Bread. After arresting him, he put him in prison, handing him over to be guarded by four squads of four soldiers each. Herod intended to bring him out for public trial after the Passover.

So Peter was kept in prison, but the church was earnestly praying to God for him.

The night before Herod was to bring him to trial, Peter was sleeping between two soldiers, bound with two chains, and sentries stood guard at the entrance. Suddenly an angel of the Lord appeared and a light shone in the cell. He struck Peter on the side and woke him up. "Quick, get up!" he said, and the chains fell off Peter's wrists.

Then the angel said to him, "Put on your clothes and sandals." And Peter did so. "Wrap your cloak around you and follow me," the angel told him. Peter followed him out of the prison, but he had no idea that what the angel was doing was really happening; he thought he was seeing a vision. They passed the first and second guards and came to the iron gate leading to the city. It opened for them by itself, and they went through it. When they had walked the length of one street, suddenly the angel left him.

Then Peter came to himself and said, "Now I know without a doubt that the Lord sent his angel and rescued me from Herod's clutches and from everything the Jewish people were anticipating."

When this had dawned on him, he went to the house of Mary the mother of John, also called Mark, where many people had gathered and were praying. Peter knocked at the outer entrance, and a servant girl named Rhoda came to answer the door. When she recognized Peter's voice, she was so overjoyed she ran back without opening it and exclaimed, "Peter is at the door!"

"You're out of your mind," they told her. When she kept insisting that it was so, they said, "It must be his angel."

But Peter kept on knocking, and when they opened the door and saw him, they were astonished. Peter motioned with his hand for them to be quiet and described how the Lord had brought him out of prison. "Tell James and the brothers about this," he said, and then he left for another place.

In the morning, there was a great commotion among the soldiers as to what had become of Peter. After Herod had a thorough search made for him and did not find him, he cross-examined the guards and ordered that they be executed.

Then Herod went from Judea to Caesarea and stayed there a while. He had been quarreling with the people of Tyre and Sidon; they now joined together and sought an audience with him. Having secured the support of Blastus, a trusted personal servant of the king, they asked for peace, because they depended on the king's country for their food supply.

On the appointed day Herod, wearing his royal robes, sat on his throne and delivered a public address to the people. They shouted, "This is the voice of a god, not of a man." Immediately, because Herod did not give praise to God, an angel of the Lord struck him down, and he was eaten by worms and died.

But the word of God continued to increase and spread.

Final Note: Luke, the first historian of the early church, recorded this story between AD 63 and AD 70.

Conclusion

My goal in writing this book is to give you a surprising taste of what the Bible has to say. I hope it whets your appetite for opening God's Word and for digging a little deeper to see how applicable it can be to your own life. It is my prayer that the stories will also create a hunger in the hearts of you readers who do not yet have a personal relationship with God, and that it will prompt you to seek after the One who loves you and has the power to bring freedom, peace, and wholeness into your life.

Anyone who examines this evidence will come to stake his life on this: that God himself is the truth.

John 3:33 MESSAGE

a ten-week study guide

Week 1

A Match Made in Heaven

Individual reflection or group discussion opener: What was the most romantic marriage proposal you ever heard of? (This could be your own story or someone you know or have read about.)

DAY ONE: Read the Story (pp. 14–22)

Who's who? Describe the following characters and what their roles were in the story:

Abraham—

Isaac—

Eliezer—

Bethuel—

Laban—

Rebekah—

DAY TWO: Read the Digging Deeper section on pages 22–29 and the Scripture reading, Genesis 24. (You may prefer to read the text from your own Bible to note the verse divisions.)

In your own words, what were the marriage customs of the day?

Why do you think Abraham didn't want his son, Isaac, to marry a Canaanite girl?

If you are single: Are there any "inappropriate" men within your circle/sphere of friends whom you know would be a wrong choice for you? Why? Have you dated him/them in the past? What was the outcome of the relationship(s)?

If you are a parent: Do you wish you could "arrange" a marriage for your child or children? Why or why not?

DAY THREE: The Power of Prayer

Consider Abraham's servant. Do you think Eliezer felt adequate for the job that his master asked of him? Why or why not?

Where did he turn for help?

What does Psalm 145:18–19 say about someone who prays?

Do you have someone who prays for you on a regular basis? If so, who?

Read Colossians 4:2. It instructs us to do three things when we pray: to be devoted or constant, to be watchful, and to be thankful. How did Eliezer model that behavior in prayer?

to be devoted/constant—

to be watchful—

to be thankful—

Eliezer's timing for arriving in the city of Nahor was perfect. Why?

What did he do upon his arrival?

Why was Abraham's servant excited when Rebekah told him who she was?

When he realized who she was, what did Eliezer do?

How many times did Eliezer stop to pray or to praise God for answered prayer in this story?

The servant asked for direction on his quest—when was the last time you sought God's direction in a particular area of your life?

Do you ask God for help on a daily basis? When was the last time you specifically saw God answer one of your prayers?

Have you thanked him for his intervention in your situation?

God provided "the right woman at the right time" in answer to Eliezer's prayer. Do you believe God still provides the right man or woman at the right time for people today? Why or why not?

Is it reasonable to think that God cares about whom we date? Or whom we choose as a mate? Have you asked for or invited his input on this matter of your life or in the lives of your children?

DAY FOUR: What's in a Name?

What did Isaac's name mean? (See p. 14)

What did Rebekah's name mean?

Rebekah in particular seemed to live up to her name. Why?

Do you know what your name means? Is it at all indicative of your personality? If so, how?

In your own words, list the personality characteristics that Rebekah might have had and why:

Rebekah agreed to marry Isaac sight unseen and to leave almost immediately with Eliezer. What did she learn about Isaac that may have prompted her decision?

Do you think Rebekah may have believed that this move was directed by God in part because she repeatedly witnessed the servant praying? What were these three occasions?

Genesis 24:12–14—

Genesis 24:26–27—

Genesis 24:50–52—

Remember that every date is a potential mate. If you are single, what characteristics are you looking for in a husband? List those things that you feel are absolutely essential.

Now list the "extras" that would be a bonus in your ideal man.

Rebekah's family was not able to plan or attend her wedding (they hadn't even met the groom!), but before she left they blessed her, saying, "Our sister, may you increase to thousands upon thousands; may your offspring possess the gates of their enemies" (Genesis 24:60). Think of someone you love; this could be your daughter, sister, or best friend. In your own words, write out the "blessing" you would like to give her on her wedding day:

DAY FIVE: The Faith Factor

How did the following characters exercise faith in this story? What action did they take?

Abraham (who did Abraham expect to guide his servant?—see Genesis 24:7)—

Isaac—

Eliezer—

Rebekah—

Rebekah's family—

Read Matthew 6:25–34. What can you learn from this Scripture about facing challenges in your life?

Take a few moments and consider an area of your life where you need to choose to exercise your faith. Do you believe that God can be trusted to help you?

What action do you need to take to put "feet to your faith"?

Week 2

Choosing to Trust

Individual reflection or group discussion opener: Who are the top two people you would turn to in a crisis and why?

DAY ONE: Read the Story (pp. 36–43)

Who were the important named and un-named characters in the story? Identify the following and explain what their roles were:

Amram—

Jochebed—

Miriam—

Aaron—

Pharaoh—

Taskmasters—

Midwives—

Pharaoh's daughter—

DAY TWO: Read the Digging Deeper section on pages 43–47 and the Scripture reading, Exodus 1:6–2:10.

In your own words, explain the setting that the Hebrew people found themselves in as our story opened (you may want to read Exodus 1–5 for extra insight).

What three things did Pharaoh do to thin out the Hebrew population?

The Hebrew people were abused and greatly misused during this time in history. Have you ever been treated unfairly in a work or social situation? If so, how did you react and what did you learn as a result of this experience?

What does Romans 5:3 say about testing?

If you faced the same unfair situation today that you referred to above, would you react in the very same way? Why or why not?

There's more to come: We continue to shout our praise even when we're hemmed in with troubles, because we know how troubles can develop passionate patience in us, and how that

215

patience in turn forges the tempered steel of virtue, keeping us alert for whatever God will do next. In alert expectancy such as this, we're never left feeling shortchanged. Quite the contrary—we can't round up enough containers to hold everything God generously pours into our lives through the Holy Spirit!

Romans 5:3–5 MESSAGE

DAY THREE: Moral and Spiritual Backbone

The midwives in our story had two face-to-face appointments with Pharaoh. At the first appointment, what assignment were they given to do?

If you had been one of the midwives, what emotions might you have experienced following your appointment with Pharaoh?

What action did the midwives take?

As a result of their disobedience, Pharaoh called in the midwives for a second face-to-face appointment, demanding to know why they hadn't obeyed his order. What was their response?

Read Exodus 1:17. Whom did the midwives fear?

All the women in this story exhibited amazing moral and/or spiritual backbone in the face of life-threatening circumstances. How did God reward them (Exodus 1:20–21)?

Have you ever been in a situation where someone in authority has asked or required you to do something that you felt was immoral, illegal, or unethical? If so, how did you react?

All of us are at different levels of spiritual maturity, and God loves us right where we are. Reflecting on your own difficult or challenging situation from your present level of maturity, do you think you would react in the same way if faced with that situation again? Why or why not?

Whom do you admire as a woman of spiritual backbone? Why do you admire her?

What actions could you take to be more like her?

DAY FOUR: An Impossible Situation

Jochebed's life was complicated by several factors. She was a slave with a condemned baby to hide, and she managed to keep the child a secret for three months. But she reached the end of her rope. Exodus 2:3 says that she reached a point when she could no longer hide him. Put yourself in her place and discuss this with your group. What were some of the challenges she may have faced during the first three months of her baby's life?

God gave this woman of faith an unusual plan that would involve two of her children. As she prepared the basket and covered it with tar and pitch, what thoughts may she have been thinking?

How do you think Miriam felt about the plan?

Luke 1:26–38 is a story about another woman of faith who chose to trust God with something that seemed impossible. Who was she?

When was the last time you took a risk knowing it was what God wanted you to do? (This could have involved a job change, a financial decision, a move, setting a healthy boundary, or releasing control of someone or something.)

Was the outcome worth the risk?

Did you involve God in your decision-making?

How soon did you recognize that God was at work in your situation?

Read the following verses and write out what the Scripture says about impossible situations:

Matthew 19:26—

Luke 1:37—

DAY FIVE: The Faith Factor

What is faith? In your own words, describe what "faith" means to you.

Hebrews 11 lists many Old Testament "Heroes of the Faith." How does Hebrews 11:1 define faith?

Read Hebrews 11:23. What does the verse say about Jochebed and Amram's state of mind?

In their desperate situation, how could the parents of Moses been anything but terrified? It's because they trusted God with their situation. It is important to remember that in choosing to trust God, Jochebed didn't put the baby afloat in the basket for an hour or so and then change her mind and snatch him back to try to manage the situation on her own. She put feet to her faith, and then she let go and allowed God to work out his plan for her family.

Isaiah 12:2 says, "Surely God is my salvation; I will trust and not be afraid. The LORD, the LORD, is my strength and my song; he has become my salvation." Do you have an impossible situation today? As a speaker, I stand before audiences filled with women who look absolutely lovely on the outside—but in truth, the vast majority of those women are struggling with major issues in their lives. For some, it's a rotten job situation, for others, an unfaithful husband, an illness, a terminally ill parent, a wayward child, a secret addiction, and the list goes on and on.

Do you realize that God loves you and has a special plan for your life? Read Jeremiah 29:11–13 aloud. God not only has a plan for your life, he listens when you pray, and if you seek him, he will be found! If we choose to trust him, he will do one of two things. He will change the situation or he will change our attitude toward the situation (which may be the far greater miracle)—or maybe both!

What is your impossible situation? This is such a personal question that you may not feel comfortable discussing it with your study group, but it is important to identify the area of greatest need in your life. (And remember that if you do decide to share your situation, your step of faith in facing this problem will be affirmed by women who will lovingly lift you and your situation to God in prayer.)

What step of faith do you need to take that would give God control of your situation? Can you pray the "Passionate Prayer" on page 47 and personalize it by talking to God about the issue you face that may seem impossible? Remember, with God, all things are possible!

Week 3

Me First, Me First!

Individual reflection or group discussion opener: Oops! Sometimes I speak before I think, and then wish I could take back what I've said. Can you recall a time when that happened to you?

DAY ONE: Read the Story (pp. 53–60)

Who's who? Who were the three main characters in the story and what were their roles?

DAY TWO: Read the Digging Deeper section on pages 61–67 and the Scripture reading, Numbers 12:1–16.

About how old was Miriam when this story took place?

Throughout her lifetime, Miriam exhibited a variety of temperaments or attitudes. (And regarding this episode, we know that she was too old for PMS to have been a factor!) How would you describe her attitude shortly after the great exodus from

Egypt began and the people had crossed the Red Sea? Why do you think she had this attitude?

What was her attitude just prior to God's intervention in this story? Why?

Read Numbers 12:3. How does it describe Moses's temperament? Does it sound as if he "lorded" his authority over Miriam and Aaron?

Describe Miriam's attitude at the end of the story and explain why it changed.

How would you describe your own temperament? Do you think that others enjoy working with you? Why or why not?

DAY THREE: Leadership Gone Awry—Who's the Boss?

God used Miriam in remarkable ways during her lifetime. How was she used of God in Exodus 2?

Read Exodus 15:20. This describes some of Miriam's abilities as a leader. She is described as a musician and dancer as she led a song of praise to the Lord, but even more notably, she is described as a "prophetess," that is, one who spoke the Word of the Lord. How many women followed Miriam at this time?

What does Micah 6:4 say about the responsibility that God had given to Miriam?

What qualities do you feel are important in a good leader?

What do you think motivates people to pursue positions of leadership?

John C. Maxwell gives readers a "Leadership Motive Check" based on 1 Peter 5:1–3, telling us that God calls us to "lead and serve voluntarily, not for selfish gain; eagerly do God's will, not to get ahead; serve as an example, not as a lord." Maxwell urges leaders to taking the following motive check:

1. When you lead, do you remember the example of Christ's sufferings? (v. 1)
2. When you shepherd, do you do it out of a sense of obligation or privilege? (v. 2)
3. When you serve, are you motivated by the will of God or men? (v. 2)
4. When you minister, are you driven by personal gain or godly passion? (v. 2)
5. When influencing others, does your life example speak clearly? (v. 3)
6. When sacrificing, can you wait for the ultimate reward, or must you see an immediate payback? (v. 3)[1]

Look up Proverbs 11:2 and write out the verse here:

What ministry do you feel that God has entrusted to you?

Are the individuals you "answer to" at work, home, and/or in ministry easy or challenging to work with? Why?

Do you pray for those in authority over you at work, home, or in ministry? Why would this be a good idea?

DAY FOUR: The Unbridled Tongue

James 1:26 says, "If anyone considers himself religious and yet does not keep a tight rein on his tongue, he deceives himself and his religion is worthless." Miriam and Aaron began to criticize Moses, God's clear choice for the leader of their people. It is interesting that they didn't choose to discuss his leadership skills, but rather they criticized something else. What did they find fault with?

What do the following verses say about malicious gossip?

Proverbs 13:3—

Proverbs 13:10—

2 Timothy 2:16—

From this story, how do you think God feels about malicious gossip?

What do you think causes people to be critical of individuals in leadership?

224

Have you ever been tempted to get caught up in talking critically about someone else?

Looking back at this ancient story, Numbers 12:4 in the Message paraphrase reads "God broke in suddenly on Moses, Aaron and Miriam" calling them out to the tent of meeting. The King James version words it slightly differently, saying, "And the Lord spoke suddenly unto Moses, and unto Aaron and unto Miriam." How would you feel if suddenly God interrupted you while you were involved in negatively criticizing someone else?

The verse (Numbers 12:4) seems to indicate that Moses was present when criticized by his siblings. How do you think he felt? Did he ask God to punish them? What did he ask God to do?

How did you respond the last time you were unjustly criticized by someone else?

DAY FIVE: The Faith Factor

Godly leaders not only have a responsibility to live a life worthy of being followed but also to be a consistent example in their faith walk with God.

God's physical presence was with the children of Israel in a tangible way—a pillar of cloud during the day and a pillar of fire at night (Exodus 13:21). To us, that sounds incredible, but in this story Miriam seems to have lost the "wow" factor. She seemed oblivious to the fact that God not only saw her actions but that he heard her criticism of Moses. Miriam tried to justify her criticism of Moses by proclaiming her own position as a prophetess.

Looking back over your life, can you recall a time when you trusted more in your own ability than in God's direction for your life?

What lesson did you learn from that episode in your life?

What does Philippians 4:13 say about our ability to succeed?

In the New Testament there is a story about a leader who took his eyes off Jesus. Read Matthew 14:22–33. What was this story about?

What things or circumstances in your life have lured your focus away from God?

What did it take, or what choices did you make (or do you need to make today), to get your faith walk back on track? Share what you learned from this experience.

Miriam was an elderly woman when this episode took place in her life. Scripture doesn't tell us what she did after her period of discipline, but we are told that the Israelites did not move on until she was restored to them. What does Titus 2:3–5 say about the life we as women should consider living?

Remember that no matter what your age, if there are women younger than you, you can be a person of influence in their lives. (A woman in her thirties can influence someone in her twenties. A woman in her twenties can influence a teenager.)

What sobering epitaph did Deuteronomy 24:9 offer regarding Miriam?

In contrast, write out 2 Timothy 4:7.

If your faith walk was evaluated and printed on your tombstone, which of the following would be the most truthful? (1) She followed after God. (2) She faltered and fell away. (3) She faltered and then faithfully followed God.

Have you allowed God to be the "boss" or Lord of your life? Can you sincerely pray the prayer at the end of Miriam's story on pages 67–68?

Week 4

Pride Takes a Bath

Individual reflection or group discussion opener: At the beginning of this chapter, there is a story about a mom being humbled by a little girl. Can you think of a time when your pride got you into an embarrassing situation?

DAY ONE: Read the Story (pp. 73–80)

Who were the important named and un-named characters in the story? Identify the following and explain what their roles were in the story:

Naaman—

The wife—

The captive—

Elisha—

Two kings—

Naaman's servants—

DAY TWO: Read the Digging Deeper section on pages 80–87 and the Scripture reading, 2 Kings 5:1–19.

Naaman was a powerful, honored, and respected military leader in a pagan land. According to 2 Kings 5:1, who was responsible for his success?

In your own words, describe Naaman's problem and how it may have affected his position.

What actions did Naaman take that indicate his situation may have been getting desperate?

Why do you think God allowed Naaman to get sick?

Do you think that God may sometimes allow difficult things to come into our lives to get us to seek him? Has adversity ever drawn you closer to God? If so, when and how?

DAY THREE: Great Expectations

What did Naaman do in preparation for his trip into enemy territory?

What did he expect from the king of Israel? What did he receive?

What did he expect upon his arrival at the prophet Elisha's home? What did he receive?

What was Naaman's response? Why do you think he responded the way he did?

What does Romans 9:20–21 say about God's response to man's rebellion?

What would have happened to Naaman if he had continued in his rebellion?

When have your expectations fallen short of what you received? What was your response?

What does Hebrews 10:35–36 say about enduring times of discouragement?

There are times when, like Naaman, we may not understand why it is so important to obey God's will. In 1 Corinthians 2:7 it says, "God's wisdom is something mysterious that goes deep within the interior of his purposes. You don't find it lying around on the surface. It's not the latest message, but more like the oldest—what God determined as the way to bring out his best in us, long before we ever arrived on the scene" (Message). What do the following Scriptures say about obeying God, and how can you apply them to your own life and situation?

Psalm 119:34–37—

1 John 5:2–5—

DAY FOUR: The Value of Wise Counsel

Every four years the president of the United States chooses his cabinet, carefully placing people around him who are men and women of experience and experts in their fields. Why do you think it is important for him to choose individuals he can trust for these positions?

Although Naaman was a powerful man, he heeded the advice of individuals around him who cared enough about him to offer wise counsel. Think back over the story of Naaman. Who gave him valuable advice in this story, and why could this action have been risky for them?

Who are the individuals in your life whom you can trust to give you wise and unselfish counsel, and are you approachable enough for them to dare to "speak truth" to you regarding specific issues in your life?

What do the following proverbs say about seeking wise advice?

Proverbs 12:15—

Proverbs 19:20—

Proverbs 15:22—

1 Kings 22:5 tells of a powerful man, the king of Judah, who instructed another powerful man, the king of Israel, to "first seek the counsel of the LORD." What does John 14:26–27 say about our most valuable Counselor?

DAY FIVE: The Faith Factor
Who was the person of faith in Naaman's household?

Read Luke 4:27. This Scripture indicates that the little girl in this story must have had remarkable faith. Why?

The child chose to be a blessing in spite of her own negative circumstances. Read Romans 12:9–15. In your own words describe how the little girl lived out the advice given in this Scripture for godly conduct.

Women today are not likely to find themselves held captive in a foreign land. However, many do find themselves captive in negative situations. Those situations could include a difficult job environment, a miserable marriage, a dysfunctional family or extended family or even church family. Have you been or are you currently caught in a difficult situation? What can you learn from the child in this story?

Naaman's physical healing and spiritual conversion are among the most dramatic in the entire Bible. Prior to obeying God's instruction, one major factor stood in the way of his new life—pride. Name at least three ways God allowed Naaman to be humbled in this story.

Naaman initially rebelled and galloped off in a rage, away from God's directive. Later, after hearing the wise advice of his servants, he made the choice to humble himself, turn around, and obey the instructions of God's servant. What do the following Scriptures say about the importance of humility?

Psalm 25:9—

James 4:10—

When Naaman humbled himself and obeyed God by following the prophet's instructions, Naaman received far more than physical healing. "His obedience opened his heart to a greater miracle than the one for which he longed."[2] He became a believer in the one true God that day. In your own words, describe the actions Naaman took that proved that he was a changed man.

Isn't it wonderful that God allows us to make U-turns in our lives? Once we turn away from our own sin and rebellion and toward him, he works a miracle in our hearts and lives. What does 2 Corinthians 5:17 say about new life in Christ, God's Son?

Do you need to make a U-turn in your life and follow after God?

If you've accepted Christ as your Savior, do others see evidence of your faith? What has changed?

Can you honestly and sincerely pray the prayer on page 87?

Week 5

Dear Abby

Individual reflection or group discussion opener: Reflecting on your past, can you name someone you dated that you are glad you didn't end up with and why?

DAY ONE: Read the Story (pp. 92–101)

Who's who? Who were the important characters in the story? Identify the following and explain what their roles were in the story:

David—

Nabal—

Abigail—

DAY TWO: Read the Digging Deeper section on pages 102–107 and the Scripture reading, 1 Samuel 25:1–42.

What did David provide for Nabal?

What did David expect from Nabal?

What did David receive from Nabal?

DAY THREE: Sleeping with the Enemy

Abigail found herself in a very difficult marital situation. In your own words, describe the character of Nabal, her husband.

The following verses refer to someone of Nabal's character. What do they say?

Proverbs 5:22—

Proverbs 17:13—

Proverbs 17:16—

Proverbs 18:6—

Proverbs 18:7—

Proverbs 19:3—

James 1:26—

How did Nabal put Abigail and his entire household at risk?

In spite of her unhappy circumstances, Abigail chose to respond with wise words and actions. In what ways did she do that?

The following verses refer to someone of Abigail's character. What do they say?

Proverbs 8:7—

Proverbs 12:18—

Proverbs 31:26—

2 Timothy 1:7—

When confronted by evil, how do you respond?

DAY FOUR: Setting Healthy Boundaries

Abigail was patient and long-suffering with Nabal until his actions threatened her entire household. At that point, she drew a line in the sand and took action that would save them all. In your own words, describe what she did to draw a healthy boundary.

The common response to injustice is anger. However, in this story Abigail acted in wisdom instead. Dr. Henry Cloud and Dr. John Townsend in their book *Boundaries* share the following: "The more biblical our boundaries are, the less anger we experience! Individuals with mature boundaries are the least angry people in the world."[3]

What do the following verses say about responding to injustice?

Proverbs 28:5—

Proverbs 3:27—

Isaiah 40:29—

Psalm 31:24—

Think about it: in what area of your life would it be wise to set a healthy boundary? (This could be at home, at work, in your extended family, etc.)

Select one of the above verses to claim for your own situation.

DAY FIVE: The Faith Factor

Abigail was beautiful physically but is known more for being a wise and godly woman. What risk did Abigail take that required great faith, and what could have resulted if she hadn't taken this step of faith?

Are you in a difficult situation? What advice does James 1:5 have for you?

Is there a lesson for you from Abigail's story? If so, what is it?

Read Proverbs 4:5–7 and write out Joshua 1:9.

Although Abigail had no idea at the time, God used a terrible crisis in her life to introduce her to her future spouse. Do you really believe that God can work all things together for good in your life? Take heart! Write out and claim Deuteronomy 31:8 for your own situation today.

Week 6

Seeking God's Face in the Rat Race of Life

Individual reflection or group discussion opener: The president was coming to our city! Admission was free, but tickets were mandatory. My husband and children were excited to attend, but upon their arrival they were directed to an outdoor parking lot where they would view the program on a jumbo outdoor screen rather than have the opportunity to see the president in person. What a disappointment!

When was the last time you found yourself at a concert, parade, or sporting event, etc., where you were unable to see or experience the event as you had hoped?

DAY ONE: Read the Story (pp. 113–17)

Who's who? Who were the two main characters in this story and what were their roles?

DAY TWO: Read the Digging Deeper section on pages 117–26 and the Scripture reading, Luke 19:1–10.

Why did his fellow Jews dislike Zacchaeus?

Do you think Zacchaeus had made a success of his life? Why or why not?

In your own words, describe why you think Zacchaeus tried so hard to see Jesus that day.

In your mind's eye, put yourself out on a limb peering through the leaves in Zacchaeus's lofty hiding place. How would you feel if Jesus stopped, looked up into your eyes, and called you by name?

DAY THREE: Who Deserves God's Forgiveness?

Have you observed a person in authority misuse his or her position for personal gain?

Zacchaeus was a well-known sinner. He had authority over his fellow Jews due to his position as the chief tax collector, but it was common knowledge that he used his job to cheat others. Read the following Scriptures. What do they tell us about how God feels about dishonesty?

Proverbs 11:1, 12—

Luke 16:10–13—

If God hates sin, why would Jesus have taken time to seek out and befriend someone like Zacchaeus when there were so many other people following him? What do the following Scriptures

241

say about who Jesus wanted to reach out to and how he felt about them?

Luke 15:1–7—

Luke 19:10—

The religious people in this story were upset that Jesus went home with Zacchaeus. If a felon recently released from prison or a local prostitute walked into your church, would they be welcomed?

Romans 3:23 says that "all have sinned and fall short of the glory of God." Bottom line, God hates sin, but he loves sinners. Why is that good news for us?

DAY FOUR: Seek and Find

Zacchaeus was a seeker, and his lonely, sinful heart longed to catch a glimpse of Jesus that day in Jericho. How little did he realize what the outcome of his actions would be! Zacchaeus did three important things that day that would change his life. For today, think about the first two of these important actions and how you might take the same action—with life-changing impact.

1. He went out of his way to see Jesus. When obstacles interrupted his plan, he came up with another. Think about it. In spite of your busy schedule, list three specific, doable actions you can take this week to consciously go out of your way to meet with Jesus.

What does Isaiah 55:6 say?

242

2. He responded immediately when Jesus called his name.
When Jesus called out to Zacchaeus and said he'd like to go home with him, Zacchaeus didn't hesitate. He didn't check his appointment book, didn't wait for the crowd to dissipate so he could climb down from the tree without people witnessing his ungainly descent, and didn't try to be politically correct in front of any Jews or Romans who might have been present. His manner and actions simply said "Yes!" to Jesus.

Do you think that God has trouble getting your attention? Why or why not?

What do you see as the biggest obstacle that keeps you from responding when God touches your heart and you know you should spend time with him?

DAY FIVE: The Faith Factor

The story of Zacchaeus is a wonderful example of a life changed dramatically when someone chose to seek, believe, and acknowledge his relationship with Jesus Christ in front of others. When the two stepped outside of Zacchaeus's home, Zacchaeus gave a public testimony of his faith in Christ but then went a step further, which gave proof to the fact that he was a changed man.

What does 2 Corinthians 5:17 say about the change that Christ works in the lives of all who believe?

Reread Luke 19:8 and in your own words describe how Zacchaeus allowed his relationship with Jesus Christ to affect his relationship with others.

243

Have you publicly acknowledged your faith in Jesus Christ? If so, what did you do and how did others react?

If you have never publicly acknowledged your faith in Jesus Christ, what would be some ways that you could do that?

Are you a seeker like Zacchaeus? Bottom line, do you need a relationship with Jesus Christ? Why not pray the prayer on page 126 and welcome the Savior into your heart and life?

In 1 Chronicles 28:9 King David gives his son Solomon advice about seeking out and serving God. It says, "acknowledge the God of your father, and serve him with wholehearted devotion and with a willing mind, for the LORD searches every heart and understands every motive behind the thoughts. If you seek him, he will be found by you."

Week 7

Faith and Friendship
Find a Way

Individual reflection or group discussion opener: Do you have a friend who would do just about anything for you? Think of an example when that friend went "beyond the call of duty" for you or your family.

DAY ONE: Read the Story (pp. 129–36)

Who's who? Jesus and a paralyzed man are the two main characters in this special story. There were two *groups* of people he dealt with as the story unfolded. Who were they?

DAY TWO: Read the Digging Deeper section on pages 136–41 and the Scripture reading, Mark 2:1–12.

Have you (or someone you're very close to) ever been handicapped, or even temporarily disabled? If so, what were your/their greatest challenges physically, emotionally, socially, or spiritually?

Did you have friends or family who rallied around you and met your needs? What did they do for you, and were you a gracious recipient of their assistance?

How would you describe the audience that Jesus was speaking to that day?

DAY THREE: Determined Friendship

In your own words, describe the challenges that the paralyzed man's friends faced in this story.

Sometimes it's challenging to befriend someone in need because it usually requires the sacrifice of time. What does Galatians 6:2 say about assisting others?

Are the spiritual needs of your friends as important to you as their physical needs? How have you tried to meet both their physical and spiritual needs?

Has there been a time when you felt the situation was hopeless, and you gave up trying to meet someone's needs? If so, what were the circumstances?

1 Corinthians 13:4 says that "love is patient, love is kind." Verse 7 says that love "always protects, always trusts, always hopes, always perseveres." In what ways have you been a de-

termined friend to someone you care about? How have you persevered?

DAY FOUR: What Does God See?

Describe what the audience saw when the mat was lowered through the hole in the ceiling that day.

What does 1 Samuel 16:7 have to say about the difference between the viewpoint of men and God?

Describe in your own words what Jesus saw that day when he looked at:

the audience in the room—

the four friends peering through the hole in the roof—

the paralytic at his feet—

Was it more important for Jesus to heal the man spiritually or physically?

When Jesus looks at you today, what do you think he sees as your greatest need?

What does Psalm 7:9 say about how God looks at us?

DAY FIVE: The Faith Factor

Mark 2:5 says that "Jesus saw their faith." Whose faith do you think he saw?

Those guys had tenacious faith, stubborn faith, determined faith, *passionate* faith. They believed that God could change their friend's life, and they were willing to overcome considerable obstacles to get him to Jesus.

Do you *believe* that God can change the lives of your friends? Are you willing to "put feet to your faith" and go out of your way to introduce her/them to Jesus Christ?

How important is our faith to God? What do Matthew 13:58 and Mark 6:5–6 indicate about its importance?

What does Hebrews 11:6 say about faith?

Who do you know who needs to meet Jesus?

What step(s) could you take to introduce her/him to the Savior?

If your friend rejects or refuses your invitation, how else could you communicate God's love to her/him?

Week 8

Look Who's
Coming to Dinner

Individual reflection or group discussion opener: What's your favorite menu to prepare if you're having company for dinner?

DAY ONE: Read the Story (pp. 145–51)

Who's who? List the important named and un-named characters in the story, and explain what their roles were.

DAY TWO: Read the Digging Deeper section on pages 151–61 and the Scripture reading, Luke 10:38–42.

What village did Martha, Mary, and Lazarus live in, and about how far was it from Jerusalem?

In your own words, describe the relationship that Jesus had with these three siblings.

List five people who would feel comfortable stopping by your house for an impromptu visit and meal.

DAY THREE: What's Cookin'?

We're not told in Scripture what food Martha prepared for this large group of guests, but we are told that she was "cumbered about with much serving." We know she couldn't order pizza or other "take out" food, but we do know that she was known for her hospitality and that Jesus and his disciples felt welcome there—that is, except for when she lost her composure in front of them all.

Do you have the gift of hospitality? Number the following in the order of most important to least important items you feel a good hostess should provide:

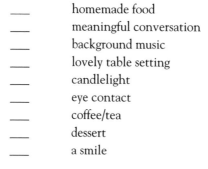

____	homemade food
____	meaningful conversation
____	background music
____	lovely table setting
____	candlelight
____	eye contact
____	coffee/tea
____	dessert
____	a smile

What do the following verses say about offering hospitality to others?

1 Peter 4:9–10—

Mark 9:41—

Romans 12:13—

Hebrews 6:10—

Hebrews 13:2—

If a large family stopped by unexpectedly right before meal-time, would you invite them to stay for dinner? If so, what would you serve?

DAY FOUR: Welcome: Women!

Matthew, Mark, and Luke, when writing about the life and ministry of Jesus Christ, all mention the fact that "many" women followed Jesus and helped to support his ministry. Although Jewish tradition discouraged the practice of women learning from rabbis, in this story we find Mary sitting on the floor near Jesus while he was teaching. When she was criticized, Jesus defended her presence there.

Read Matthew 27:55; Mark 5:41; Mark 15:41; Luke 8:1–3; Luke 24:1; and John 4:27. These passages all refer to women and Jesus. In your own words, describe why you think women loved, followed, and supported his ministry.

In some parts of the world today, women are still considered inferior or unworthy of education or of voicing their opinion. In your mind's eye, put yourself in their place and consider how you would feel if you met Jesus on the street and he took time to speak to you and then reached out and changed your life drastically for the better by healing your sick child. How would you feel? What would you do?

Jesus Christ is still in the life changing business. Has he changed your life? If so, how?

Do you love, follow, and support the ministry of Jesus Christ? If so, how?

Brainstorm for a moment about how you personally can do more to support the cause of Christ and how you can encourage other women to do the same.

DAY FIVE: The Faith Factor

Because Jesus and his followers were controversial, there was risk involved with meeting together. This, no doubt, heightened the excitement of their visits and added tension for the home-owner. In this story, Martha exercises her faith by welcoming Jesus and his disciples to her home. Mary exhibits her faith by sitting at Jesus's feet with the men in the room and listening to Jesus's teaching.

Romans 12:6–8 describes a number of spiritual gifts and urges us to use our gift "in proportion to [our] faith." What gifts are listed?

Can you identify one of the gifts listed as your own? If so, what is it and how are you using it for Jesus's sake?

What was Martha's spiritual gift?

If she was exercising her gift, what got her into trouble? In your own words, describe what you think she did wrong.

Can you remember a time when you worked hard in preparation for a family gathering and ended up in tears before the "happy" gathering was over? Thinking back to a few of those awkward episodes in my life, I realize in hindsight that several scenarios were likely: I had worked myself to a frazzle prior to my guests' arrival, I hadn't delegated food or activity assignments very well, other relatives didn't pitch in to help like I thought they should, my expectations were too great, or I was trying to impress my guests rather than to make their visit joyful. When was the last time something like that happened to you, and would you do anything differently if you could live the day all over again?

Jesus loved Martha enough to hold her accountable for her attitude and actions that evening. The result was life changing, and we see a whole new Martha in John 11 and 12, which we will explore next week. Bottom line, she learned from her mistakes and went on to give a passionate statement of faith in the face of deep disappointment, and she continued to serve Christ and others.

Are you passionate about serving God and about sharing your faith with others?

Is your home an open place where the company and conversation is loving and honoring to God? When guests come to your house, are they more impressed with your genuine warmth or with the food you serve or the table service you use?

Can you sincerely pray the prayer on pages 161–62?

Week 9

"You're Late, God!
Where Were You When
I Needed You?"

Individual reflection or group discussion opener: What was the most meaningful funeral you ever attended? What made it special?

DAY ONE: Read the Story (pp. 165–70)

Who's who? Name the four main characters and explain what their roles were in the story.

DAY TWO: Read the Digging Deeper section on pages 170–79 and the Scripture reading, John 11:1–45.

Why were Martha and Mary discouraged and disillusioned in this story?

DAY THREE: Politics and Religion

Why was it risky for Jesus to show up in Bethany after Lazarus died?

Do you think Jesus waited to come to the aid of his friends because of the risk involved? Why or why not?

What were the two major Jewish religious groups and why didn't they welcome Jesus?

According to the following verses, how did religious leaders try to discredit Jesus?

Matthew 9:10–12—

Matthew 9:32–34—

Matthew 12:1–2—

Matthew 12:9–10—

Matthew 12:22–24—

Matthew 21:43–45—

Do you feel that there are religious groups today who oppose the cause of Christ and misuse their authority for political purposes?

255

Often Jesus refused to make a "show" of miracles (Matthew 12:38–39) for religious leaders. In Matthew 7:1–6, Jesus instructed on how to deal with troublemakers. In your own words, how would you summarize his advice?

DAY FOUR: Heartache and Disillusionment

What did Martha and Mary expect when they sent a message to Jesus?

What was Jesus's response?

Do you think their request was reasonable, given their close friendship with Jesus? Why or why not?

Both sisters struggled with disillusionment. It seemed to them that Jesus had ignored their cry for help. If he truly loved them, why did he wait to come? Do you think Jesus understood their grief and disillusionment? If yes, why?

Philip Yancey, in his book *Where Is God When It Hurts?*, writes, "Human suffering remains meaningless and barren unless we have some assurance that God is sympathetic to our pain and can somehow heal that pain. In Jesus, we have that assurance."[4] What do the following verses say about heartache and suffering?

Psalm 27:14—

Psalm 126:5–6—

John 14:1—

John 14:27—

Revelation 21:4—

Have you ever struggled with disappointment with God? If so, as time passed, did you via hindsight gain any understanding regarding "why" God allowed what happened in your situation or how God worked through the situation to bring about good in your life?

I am convinced that there are some questions I will only have answered in heaven, but the comment below, by someone who has studied suffering, is comforting.

Suffering can be what economists call a "frozen asset." It may not look remotely like an asset at the time, but gradually we can find meaning in it, an enduring meaning that will help to transform the pain.[5]

Martha and Mary found their sorrow turned to joy sooner than they expected—and their experience gave evidence to the fact that Jesus had power over death itself before he himself died and then rose again.

DAY FIVE: The Faith Factor

Jesus was well known for healing the sick, yet he "allowed" his dear friends to experience the heartache of Lazarus's death.

It was enough to shake the sisters' faith. And yet, when they realized Jesus had come, they still went to him separately and poured out their anguish to him. What an important message for us! What do the following verses say about how or when we should approach God?

Psalm 55:4–5, 16—

Psalm 55:22—

1 Peter 5:6–7—

Proverbs 3:5–6—

Hebrews 4:16—

At the instant of pain, it may seem impossible to imagine that good can come from tragedy. (It must have seemed so to Christ at Gethsemane.) We never know in advance exactly how suffering can be transformed into a cause for celebration. But that is what we are asked to believe. Faith means believing in advance what will only make sense in reverse.[6]

Although both Martha and Mary said, "Lord, if you'd been here my brother would not have died," Martha had a conversation with Jesus that resulted in her declaration of faith that is one of the clearest in the Bible. Write out her declaration from John 11:27.

Later, standing at the grave site, Jesus reminded her that if she believed, she would see the glory of God that day (John 11:40). Moments later, her brother was raised from the dead. Are you struggling with grief or deep disappointment? Take a moment to identify an area of your life where you struggle with disappointment.

Once this is identified, go to God and unload your heartache on him, remembering that he deeply cares for you and about your situation. Can you honestly pray the prayer on page 179?

Instead of asking God "why" regarding your disappointment, choose to ask him to use your situation to bring glory to God and to point you in the direction he wants you to go.

Run to Jesus—and cry. Run to Jesus—and laugh. Run to Jesus—and live.

Week 10

Escape from Death Row!

Individual reflection or group discussion opener: Do you believe in the power of prayer? What was the most exciting answer to prayer that you've ever experienced?

DAY ONE: Read the Story (pp. 184–91)

Who's who? Who were the important characters in the story? Identify the following and explain what their roles were in the story:

King Herod—

Peter—

Mary—

Rhoda—

Prayer vigil attendees—

DAY TWO: Read the Digging Deeper section on pages 191–202 and the Scripture reading, Acts 12:1–24.

What were the coliseums used for during this period of history?

What is the biggest stadium or arena you've ever been seated in? What attracted the crowd to the stadium that day?

In this story, what event was planned by Herod to entertain the crowds?

DAY THREE: In the Clutches of the Enemy

Who was King Herod's grandfather, and what terrible deed was he known for?

Why had Peter been arrested, and what did Herod plan to do to him?

How many guards were assigned to watch Peter?

Peter was in a desperate situation. No doubt he took comfort from Scriptures he had studied and committed to memory. How would the following Scriptures have comforted him?

Psalm 23:6—

Psalm 31:23–24—

Joshua 1:9—

Proverbs 14:32—

In your mind's eye, imagine yourself in Peter's predicament. You are to be tried and executed tomorrow. What do you wish you still had time to do?

Do you realize that you have an enemy?

DAY FOUR: The Power of Prayer

While Peter slept on a damp prison floor, some faithful friends had gathered to pray for him nearby. We know that both men and women and at least one child attended that passionate prayer meeting, and that it stretched far into the night. To their shock, God answered their prayers! In your own words, describe how their prayers were answered.

Do you believe that God answers prayer? What do the following Scriptures say about prayer?

Psalm 50:15—

Psalm 145:18–19—

God not only delivered Peter from Herod's clutches, but he also destroyed Herod. What happened to him?

How often do you pray?

What events have prompted you to intense prayer in the past year?

Are you open to a new way to pray? Plan a "prayer walk." Go for a walk with the specific purpose of spending time alone with God, and talk with him as you walk, offering praise and thanksgiving for his creation around you. Open up to him about the cares that are on your heart. If a friend or relative can join you, take turns quietly praying out loud as you walk with God. Thank God for how he has answered prayers in the past. If you can't physically get out, plan another way to spend time with God in prayer. (It's your powerful secret weapon against the enemy!)

___

DAY FIVE: The Faith Factor

When we choose to trust him, God will do one of two things. He will either change our circumstances (he is God, after all) or he will change our attitude regarding our circumstances (which may be the far greater miracle)—or he will do both.

Before Peter was delivered from his chains, the Scripture says he fell asleep. Amazing! How could he have been calm enough to sleep soundly? Look up the following verses about the peace that is available to all those who have put their faith in God.

Psalm 4:8—

Psalm 145:13—

Isaiah 26:3–4—

Philippians 4:7—

Do you realize that as a believer you have access to God's peace? Each of us can go to him and exchange our fear or weakness for his strength and his peace.

Peter was bound physically by the enemy. Many of us are bound in other ways by the enemy. Choose one of the above verses to claim in your own situation. And remember that God invites us to cast our cares upon him.

Will you allow God to use this ten-week study of his Word to increase your faith? Can you pray the closing prayer on page 203? If you feel that your faith is weak, consider asking God to take what faith you have and to make it enough. Become a woman of *passionate* faith.

Notes

Chapter 1: A Match Made in Heaven

1. Dr. Bruce H. Wilkinson, *The Prayer of Jabez* (Sisters, Ore.: Multnomah Publishers, 2000), 21.

2. Ralph Gower, *The New Manners and Customs of Bible Times* (Chicago: Moody Press, 1987), 236–37.

3. Ibid., 54.

Chapter 2: Choosing to Trust

1. Source unknown.

2. Original source of the story unknown. Basic idea was embellished by the author of this book!

Chapter 3: Me First, Me First!

1. Rabbi Joseph Telushkin, *Biblical Literacy* (New York: William Morrow and Company, 1997), 130.

2. This story also appears in Carol Kent's *Mothers Have Angel Wings* (Colorado Springs: NavPress, 1997).

3. Walter Elwell, *Baker Commentary on the Bible* (Grand Rapids: Baker, 1989), 86.

Chapter 4: Pride Takes a Bath

1. A. R. Fausset, *Fausset's Bible Dictionary* (Grand Rapids: Zondervan, 1981), 430.

2. Bruce Wilkinson and Kenneth Boa, *Talk Thru the Old Testament* (Nashville: Thomas Nelson, 1983), 92.

Chapter 5: *Dear Abby*

1. Susan Hunt, *Spiritual Mothering* (Wheaton, Ill.: Crossway Books, 1992), 146.
2. *Our Daily Bread* (Grand Rapids: RBC Ministries), date and author unknown.

Chapter 6: *Seeking God's Face in the Rat Race of Life*

1. Source unknown.
2. John Powell, *Why Am I Afraid to Tell You Who I Am?* (Allen, Tex.: Thomas More, 1993), 11.
3. Gower, *The New Manners and Customs of Bible Times*, 178.
4. This quote is taken from a study note on tax collectors from the Jobs and Occupations index in *The Word in Life Study Bible* (Nashville: Thomas Nelson, 1996), 2449.

Chapter 8: *Look Who's Coming to Dinner*

1. Original source of story unknown. Basic idea was embellished by the author of this book!
2. Dr. Herbert Lockyer, *All the Women of the Bible* (Grand Rapids: Zondervan, 1988).
3. Jeanne W. Hendricks, *A Woman for All Seasons* (Nashville: Thomas Nelson, 1977), 152.
4. Gower, *The New Manners and Customs of Bible Times*, 2427.
5. This quote is taken from a study note for Luke 23:49 in *The Word in Life Study Bible*, 1846.
6. Randy Alcorn, "Can't You See That I'm Busy?" *Moody*, October 1984, 36.
7. Matthew Henry, *Matthew Henry's Commentary on the Whole Bible* (Marshallton, Del.: The National Foundation for Christian Education, 1845), 397.

Chapter 9: *"You're Late, God! Where Were You When I Needed You?"*

1. This quote is taken from a study note for Matthew 26:3–5 in *The Word in Life Study Bible*, 1693.
2. This quote is taken from a study note for John 12:1–8 in *The Word in Life Study Bible*, 1894.
3. This quote is taken from a study note for Luke 9:51 in *The Student Bible*, New International Version (Grand Rapids: Zondervan, 1986), 1077.
4. Henry, *Matthew Henry's Commentary on the Whole Bible*, 607.
5. Dee Brestin and Kathy Troccoli, *Falling in Love with Jesus* (Nashville: Word, 2000), 32.
6. Ibid., 173.
7. Carol Kent, *Secret Longings of the Heart* (Colorado Springs: NavPress, 1997), 204.

Chapter 10: *Escape from Death Row!*

1. Lockyer, *All the Women of the Bible*, 141.
2. *Life Application Bible*, New International Version (Wheaton: Tyndale House and Grand Rapids: Zondervan, 1991), 1974.
3. A. T. Robertson, *Word Pictures in the New Testament* (Grand Rapids: Baker, 1990), quoted at http://bible.crosswalk.com
4. Ibid.
5. Henry, *Matthew Henry's Commentary on the Whole Bible*, vol. 3, 803.
6. *The Word in Life Study Bible*, 1921.
7. This quote is taken from a study note for Acts 12:5 in *Life Application Bible*, New International Version, 1974.
8. Quin Sherrer and Ruthanne Garlock, *A Woman's Guide to Spiritual Warfare* (Ann Arbor, Mich.: Servant Publications, 1991), 33–34.
9. J. Vernon McGee, *Acts Chapters 1–14* (Nashville: Thomas Nelson, 1991), 139.

A Ten-Week Study Guide

1. John Maxwell, *The Maxwell Leadership Bible* (Nashville: Thomas Nelson, 2002), 1534.
2. Ann Spangler and Robert Wolgemuth, *Men of the Bible* (Grand Rapids: Zondervan, 2002), 231.
3. Dr. Henry Cloud and Dr. John Townsend, *Boundaries* (Grand Rapids: Zondervan, 1992), 115.
4. Philip Yancey, *Where Is God When It Hurts* (Grand Rapids: Zondervan, 1990), 156.
5. Ibid., 200–201.
6. Ibid., 157.

As a motivational speaker, trainer, and storyteller, **Jennie Afman Dimkoff** speaks throughout the U.S. and Canada for conferences and retreats. She is the president of Storyline Ministries, Inc., and the author and storyteller for *Kids' Time*, a children's audio-cassette ministry. Jennie also serves on the staff of Speak Up With Confidence seminars.

Married to her best friend, probate court judge Graydon W. Dimkoff, Jennie is "Mom" to their two grown children, Amber and Josh. She believes that the Christian woman should choose to be God's woman in every phase of life and is committed to serving as a Christian leader in her community and beyond. She serves as a board committee member for Gerber Memorial Hospital and for the Dogwood Center for the Performing Arts, and she serves on the board of trustees of Cornerstone University. She was the first chairperson for the first Christian Women's Club in Newaygo County, Michigan, and served four years as an area representative for Stonecroft Ministries, among other church and community activities.

Jennie is a member of the National Speakers' Association and has been a keynote speaker at arena events, including Heritage Keepers and Time Out for Women. In conference and retreat settings, whether large or small, her in-depth teaching is generously seasoned with her gifted storytelling, leaving audiences greatly entertained, deeply moved, and highly motivated.

Jennie is represented by Speak Up Speaker Services. For information on scheduling her to speak for your organization, contact:

Speak Up Speaker Services
Call toll-free: (888) 870-7719
Email: speakupinc@aol.com
www.speakupspeakerservices.com

Respected Teacher
Makes Bible Stories *Come Alive*

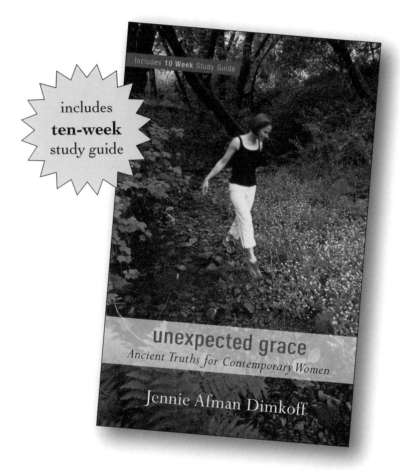

includes
ten-week
study guide

Includes **10 Week** Study Guide

unexpected grace
Ancient Truths for Contemporary Women

Jennie Afman Dimkoff

with practical application
for today's woman

 Revell
www.revellbooks.com